Off-Street Paved Bike Paths in Oregon

Oregon's Multi-Use Path Guide

Rick Bronson

D0206619

Off-Street Paved Bike Paths in Oregon: Oregon's Multi-Use Path Guide
by Rick Bronson

Second (2.454) Edition
PedalPals Press

5050 Donald St.
Eugene, OR 97405
USA
http://www.pedalpals.com/

Edited by Betsy Bronson
Front cover pictures: Main: Silver Falls State Park
Left inset: Seaside
Right inset: Willamette Greenway Trail, West Bank, North Part
Back cover pictures clockwise from top-left:
Midge Cramer
Willamette Mission State Park
Row River (photo by Joe Blakely)
The Historic Columbia River Highway State Trail #2
Riverfront Path (Corvallis)
Marine Drive #3
Bear Creek Greenway #2

ISBN: 0-9717571-0-0
for book corrections see: http://www.pedalpals.com/

NOTE: Two new paths were found after this book printed
1. Canby Logging Road Trail (2.1 miles).
   Getting there: Parking lot (not signed) at Territorial Road
   and N. Forest Ct. in Canby.
2. Weyerhaeuser Truck Rd. (Logging Road) Cottage Grove
   (London Rd area). Need visitor's permit, call 541-741-5324

Published 2005

Dedication

This book is dedicated to my family who have endured a great amount dealing with my love, infatuation, obsession, and idiosyncrasies with anything bicycle.

Table of Contents

Forward .... **vii**

    Overview Map vii
    Path Criteria viii
    Path Uses viii
    Demand ix
    Path Safety x
    Book Purpose xi
    Bicycling Safety xi
    Map Legend xiii
    Disclaimer xiii

Part 1. Portland Metro **1**

    1 Banks-Vernonia State Trail 2
    2 Forest Grove Hwy 47 6
    3 Brookwood 8
    4 Willow Creek Trail/Waterhouse Powerline Trail 10
    5 Beaverton Powerline Trail, North 13
    6 Murrayhill Powerline Park, South 16
    7 Fanno Creek Park, North 19
    8 Fanno Creek Park, South 22
    9 Forest Glen Parkway 25
    10 Summer Lake Park 27
    11 Oregon Electric ROW Trail and Linear Park 29
    12 Springwater Corridor 31
    13 I-205 34
    14 I-84 37
    15 Peninsula Crossing 39
    16 Marine Drive #1 42
    17 Marine Drive #2 45
    18 Marine Drive #3 47
    19 Marine Drive #4 50
    20 Willamette Greenway Trail, West Bank, North Part 53
    21 Willamette Greenway Trail, West Bank, South Part 56
    22 Willamette River, East Bank 59
    23 Kruse Way 62
    24 Tryon Creek State Park 64
    25 Tualatin River Greenway, Cook Park 67
    26 Faraday Lane 70

27 Columbia River Waterfront Trail/Tidewater Cove Trail 73
28 Salmon Creek Greenway Trail 76
29 Discovery Trail West 79
30 Discovery Trail East 82

Part 2. Oregon Coast **84**

31 Ft. Stevens State Park 85
32 Astoria Riverwalk 88
33 Seaside Promenade 90
34 Nehalem Bay State Park 93
35 South Beach State Park 96

Part 3. Mid Willamette Valley **98**

36 Champoeg State Park 99
37 Rickreall to Monmouth 102
38 Willamette Mission State Park 104
39 Salem Parkway 107
40 Salem Hwy 22 110
41 Minto-Brown Island Park 112
42 Silver Falls State Park 115
43 Periwinkle Bike Path 118
44 West Corvallis 121
45 Riverfront Path 124
46 Campus Way/Midge Cramer 126
47 Corvallis Hwy 99 129

Part 4. South Willamette Valley **131**

48 Roosevelt Blvd/Beltline 132
49 Willamette River Trail-West 135
50 Willamette River Trail-East 138
51 Fern Ridge Trail 141
52 Amazon Trail 143
53 By-Gully Bike & Jogging Path 146
54 Pioneer Parkway 148
55 Springfield EWEB 151
56 Booth Kelly Logging Road 153
57 Row River 155

Part 5. South Oregon **158**

58 Roseburg I-5 159
59 Roseburg Riverfront Path 161
60 John Dellenback Trail 164

61 Joseph Stewart State Park 167
62 Bear Creek Greenway #1 170
63 Bear Creek Greenway #2 173
64 Ashland... 176
65 Klamath A Canal / Kit Carson... 178
66 OC&E Woods Line State Trail... 181

Part 6. East Oregon... **184**

67 The Historic Columbia River Highway State Trail #1 185
68 Viento State Park.. 188
69 The Historic Columbia River Highway State Trail #2 191
70 The Dalles Riverfront Trail #1 193
71 The Dalles Riverfront Trail #2 196
72 The Dalles Riverfront Trail #3 199
73 Umatilla River Parkway... 202
74 Madras Willow Creek.. 204
75 Juniper Hills Park.. 206
76 Eagle Crest... 208
77 Dry Canyon... 211
78 Prineville 214
79 Leo Adler Memorial Pathway 216
80 Bend 219
81 Sunriver Resort 221
82 Crescent 223

Glossary... **225**
A. Maps, Resources **227**
B. Distance Chart **233**

Forward

This book is a collection of all paved off-road bike paths intended for non-motorized use, sometimes called multi-use paths(see glossary), in the State of Oregon that are 1 mile and over in length. These paths are used by bicyclists, inline skaters, walkers, skaters, joggers, wheelchairs, runners, and skateboarders. Even though multi-use paths support all of these modes, this book was written primarily for bicyclists.

Overview Map

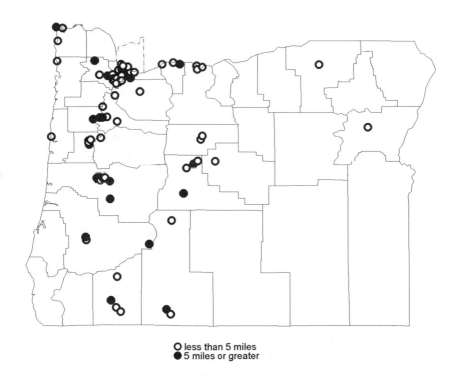

O less than 5 miles
● 5 miles or greater

This book's intended audience are those people who, for whatever reason, like paved road cycling but don't like to be near motorized traffic. There are a wide variety of reasons not to like motorized traffic, some of which include: noise, breathing pollution from passing traffic, safety, coming close to a moving vehicle of 2000 pounds, road rage, etc. They probably were road bikers at one time but due to a variety of factors like the increase in the number and size of motorized vehicles on the road and the corresponding decrease in the number of bicycles on the road they just don't feel very comfortable or safe riding among motorized traffic.

A well designed path provides a riding environment that can't be duplicated on a street. The careful street cyclist needs to be cognizant of every auto that passes. On many streets, this has the effect of wearing the rider out and he/she has trouble enjoying the other aspects of a ride such as the scenery. A path provides a less stressful riding experience where one can enjoy the surroundings and concentrate more on cycling, rather than "defensive cycling".

A path also provides cleaner air for the bicyclist. The American Lung Association [1] recommends avoiding exercise near high-traffic areas. These days, many streets are considered "high-traffic".

Path Criteria

The criteria used in this book to determine if a given path is suitable for inclusion are as follows. It must be paved with asphalt, concrete, chip seal, or sand seal and be one mile or greater in length and eight feet or wider in width. It must be physically separated from a road by at least a curb.

In this first edition, I decided to put as many paths in the book as possible to get feedback as to what readers like and don't like. Later editions may increase the length criteria or add a maximum number of conflicts per distance. It might also be prudent to eliminate widened sidewalks that cross many driveways and streets. Many of these are dangerous.

Instead of treating a network of paths as a single path, I tried to break them up logically. In some cases, like I205 and Springwater trail, it was easy. These two trails have little to do with each other, they just happen to cross. In other cases, like Eugene's Willamette River Trails, it was difficult. They are big enough that it's hard to treat them as one entity so they were broken in half.

Path Uses

These multi-use paths have three general uses: recreational, commuting, and business. Most of us can identify with the recreational aspects of a multi-use path, a strip of concrete meandering through a park is essentially a multi-use path. If this path stretches from an office park or shopping area to a housing area, then this path also serves as as commuter path. These commuter paths can really add to the livability of a city as they tend to reduce the number of auto trips that are made, thereby lowering pollution and congestion. How can a multi-use path be used by businesses? Just as roads are used by businesses so too can multi-use paths. A company called Peddlers Express in Eugene was started in 1992 to deliver packages and newspapers to area businesses using only human powered machines and continues to make money today. They make extensive use of the multi-use paths in and around Eugene.

Demand

There has never been a greater demand for multi-use paths than today. Many people are asking their cities, counties and states to build them. According to *Tualatin Hills Trails Master Plan* "When asked to prioritize planning actions for the future, expanding the off-street trail/bikeway system ranked #2." In *Moving Ahead: The American Public Speaks on Roadways and Transportation in Communities* [2] a survey identified Bikeways, Paths, and Sidewalks as the second most important factor in deciding where to live by transportation users. Some see them as the only hope for an alternative to the oppressive car-culture of this country. They envision a whole system of them linking communities much like the expressway system for motorized traffic.

Population has increased dramatically in Oregon in the past few decades with an increasing demand for more outdoor recreational facilities and more alternative transportation options. Lots of people would like to commute to work or the grocery store but they refuse to do it on crowded city streets. The average miles traveled per person annually by auto was 4570 miles in 1965. By 1995 it had exploded to 9220 miles per person per year! [3] The average size of a vehicle has increased dramatically during the nineties due to greater sales of SUV's and trucks. These two factors have tended to "crowd out" bicycles and pedestrians from city streets. Non-motorized traffic tends to feel less safe when there is either too much motorized traffic or the vehicles around them are too big. If this isn't bad enough, the increase in competition for road space has led to a lot of irritable drivers (road rage being the extreme case) which tends to scare bicyclists off the road and pedestrians off the sidewalks.

Path Safety

Another factor in this whole equation is bicycling safety. Auto safety has made very impressive gains in the past 5 decades while bike and pedestrian safety has stood at a virtual standstill. Indeed, one of the only safety advancements in the 100+ years of bicycling has been the helmet. The advancements in auto safety tend to make people believe they need to be in a modern car rather than on a bicycle to be safe on the road. The result of this is that bicycles and pedestrians feel safe on multi-use paths but they don't feel safe in traffic. The State of Oregon apparently doesn't agree with this as they openly promote Route 101 as the "Oregon Coast Bike Route", a road with over 10,000 vehicles per day during the summer months, when most bicyclists use it!

Safety comes in two forms, real safety backed up with reliable statistics and perceived safety. Real safety statistics on bicycles are hard to come by and sometimes seem to be contradictory. For example, Failure Analysis Associates Inc. [4] reports that you're 1.8 times more likely to die riding in a car as pedaling a bike (as measured by time) but the U.S. Department of Transportation [5] states that bicycling has either 10 times (measured per distance) or about 3 times (measured per trip) the fatality rate as the automobile. It's seems logical to measure risk rates by time but I'm not convinced any of these statistics are very accurate. How people perceive bicycle safety is easy. Bicycles are very dangerous, much more so than motorized vehicles. This perception is responsible for most of the 50% drop in bicycle ridership that occurred between 1977 and 1995. Thankfully, there are efforts underway to address this problem by the U.S. Department of Transportation and the Center for Disease Control, which recognize the health risks with sedentary lifestyles.

There has been a raging debate on bike path safety or lack thereof, mostly in mailing lists and newsgroups on the Internet. One camp [6] holds that bike paths are more dangerous and that governments know this but use the public perception that they are safer. They have statistics that show that bike paths are more dangerous than riding your bike on the streets alongside motorized traffic. This group also worries that misguided officials will ban bicycles on streets and force them on the more dangerous paths. The other camp sees bike paths as a safe haven from the behemoths of the road, where they breathe easy, far from the noxious gases of these dreaded monstrosities. These paths are so safe, they let their kids ride these paths totally unsupervised.

Reality is somewhere between these two groups. It's true that some very poorly designed paths (including some in this book!) are probably more dangerous than street riding. Typically, these paths have a lot of conflicts (see glossary) and are usually widened sidewalks running along busy streets or highways with just a curb separating them from the actual road. On the other hand, there are paths with virtually no conflicts and the endpoints are correctly designed to make getting on and off as safe as possible. These paths are very safe compared with a typical city street.

Book Purpose

My reasons for writing this book are twofold. The primary reason is to provide a collection of all multi-use paths in the State of Oregon. To my knowledge, no one has attempted this. There are many collections of mountain bike trails, on-road bike trails (Oregon Coast Bike Route, for instance) and hiking trails but nothing for those of us who prefer road bike conditions but without motorized traffic. Secondarily, I hope this book inspires all those interested to become involved in local, state, and national bicycle organizations to try to convince those leaders to increase the infinitesimal amount of money being spent on multi-use paths. Most of the money for these multi-use paths comes from the Transportation Efficiency Act (TEA) and this is a very limited fund. If a multi-use path is adjacent to a road, it may be eligible for funding from road tax which is a much bigger pot of money. Unfortunately, this has led to paths that are very close to big and very noisy roads, like I-205 through Portland and I-5 in Eugene. While you can argue "at least they were built", I often wonder how many people are willing to bike in an environment of 90 decibel traffic noise. If at all possible, it's best to build paths either along rivers, creeks, or streams or through quiet neighborhoods.

Bicycling Safety

Riders of these paths should familiarize themselves with the "Oregon

Bicyclists's Manual" [7] which lists four basic principles

- Maintain control of your bicycle
- Ride on the right, with traffic, in a predictable manner.
- Be visible and ride alertly.
- Protect yourself: wear a helmet to reduce the risk of head injury in the event of a crash.

The laws that apply to bicycle paths are the same laws that apply to bicycle use on sidewalks: [8]

Basic rules of the sidewalk for bicyclists are contained in ORS 814.410 which provides as follows: [9]

814.410. Unsafe operation of bicycle on sidewalk; penalty.

1. A person commits the offense of unsafe operation of a bicycle on a sidewalk if the person does any of the following:

   a. Operates the bicycle so as to suddenly leave a curb or other place of safety and move into the path of a vehicle that is so close as to constitute an immediate hazard.

   b. Operates a bicycle upon a sidewalk and does not give an audible warning before overtaking and passing a pedestrian and does not yield the right of way to all pedestrians on the sidewalk.

   c. Operates a bicycle on a sidewalk in a careless manner that endangers or would be likely to endanger any person or property.

   d. Operates the bicycle at a speed greater than an ordinary walk when approaching or entering a crosswalk, approaching or crossing a driveway or crossing a curb cut or pedestrian ramp and a motor vehicle is approaching the crosswalk, driveway, curb cut or pedestrian ramp. This paragraph does not require reduced speeds for bicycles either:

      A. At places on sidewalks or other pedestrian ways other than places where the path for pedestrians or bicycle traffic approaches or crosses that for motor vehicle traffic; or

      B. When motor vehicles are not present.

e. Operates an electric assisted bicycle on a sidewalk.

2. Except as otherwise specifically provided by law, a bicyclist on a sidewalk or in a crosswalk has the same rights and duties as a pedestrian on a sidewalk or in a crosswalk.

3. The offense described in this section, unsafe operation of a bicycle on a sidewalk, is a Class D traffic infraction.

Riders of paths should be extra careful at conflict points, especially driveway crossings, street and highway crossings, and points of entry and exit to the path. These locations provide the greatest possibility for a bad accident. Also be very careful of pedestrians.

Map Legend

Map Legend

⬭⬭⬭⬭⬭	Bike path	▬▬▬	Primary Hwy
– – – –	Trail	▬▬▬	Stream
———	City street	▬▬▬	Shoreline
▬▬▬	Secondary Hwy	⊢—⊢—	Railroad

⚑	School	🚗	Parking
⚒	Bikeshop	🚹🚺	Restroom
🚰	Water		

Forward

Disclaimer

The author and PedalPals make no claims about the safety or fitness of the paths covered in this book. The author has ridden every path but makes no claims as the accuracy of the information contained within and the suitability of the paths for any purpose and disclaims any responsibility for any harm cause by the use of these paths.

Notes

1. *American Lung Association Fact Sheet: Particulate Matter Air Pollution* (http://www.lungusa.org/air/pm_factsheet99.html)

2. *Moving Ahead: The American Public Speaks on Roadways and Transportation in Communities* (http://www.fhwa.dot.gov/reports/movingahea

3. *The Amicus Journal Summer* 1999, p. 22

4. *Comparative Risk of Different Activities, Design News, October 4, 1993* (http://www.magma.ca/~ocbc/comparat.html)

5. *Making Walking and Cycling Safer: Lessons from Europe* (http://policy.rutgers.edu/papers/10.pdf)

6. *John Forester* (http://www.johnforester.com/)

7. *Oregon Bicyclist's Manual* (http://www.odot.state.or.us/techserv/bikewa manual/)

8. *Oregon Statutes Pertaining to Bicycles and Pedestrians* (http://www.odot.state.or.us/techserv/bikewalk/plan_app/statutes.htm)

9. *Swanson Thomas & Coon - Attorneys at Law* (http://www.stc-law.com/bikemulti.html)

Part 1. Portland Metro

Portland was voted the best bicycling city in 2001 by Bicycling Magazine and the bike paths have a lot to do with the award. Portland has it all, from urban paths along the Willamette River to quiet rural paths that aren't too far from the city.

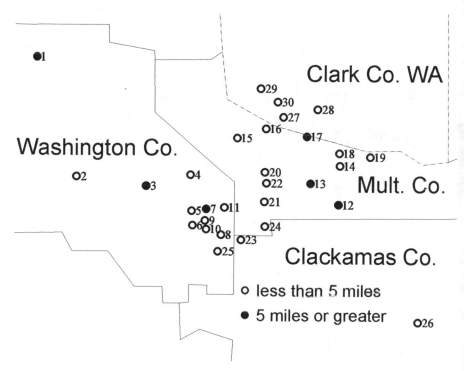

1 Banks-Vernonia State Trail

Table 1-1. Path Data

Distance	Cities	Counties	Map	End1	End2
13.6 mi.	Banks, Vernonia	Washington, Columbia	U	Banks	Vernonia

Table 1-2. Path Data

Setting	Path Surface	Internet
Rail to Trail	8 ft Asphalt, gravel	*http://www.oregonstateparks.org*

Picnicking at Buxton Trestle

Getting There: From Portland, take Highway 26 west for about 50 miles. About a half mile past Highway 6, go west on Banks Road for 1 mile, turn left (south) on Highway 47 and park in Banks. Alternatively, continue on Highway 26 and go north on Highway 47 and go to one of the trailheads (see map).

This is a gem of a path and actually a state park. Starting in a beautiful valley made by the West Fork of Dairy Creek near Banks, it heads north through lovely forests to Vernonia, following an abandoned section of the old Spokane Portland Seattle Railway. The path has a very slight uphill grade to about the halfway point then a very slight downhill grade to Vernonia. Along the way, you will pass some primarily agriculture areas and some very lush forests. The only downside to this path is that it's not completely paved and one and a half miles of it is on a gravel road due to a property dispute.

Starting in Banks, the path is made up of alternating paved and non-paved segments. Specifically, 3.3 miles paved, 1.6 gravel, 1.5 paved, 7.4 gravel, and finally 8.7 paved ending at Lake Vernonia, known locally as the Mill Pond. If you begin your trip in Banks, there is no parking near the actual beginning of the path which is at 15028 NW Highway 47, 0.6 miles north of Banks on Hwy 47. The closest place to park is 0.2 miles north of Banks along the side of busy Hwy 47. Alternatively, you can park in the town of Banks and pedal the little more than half mile to the path start. If you just want to do the longest paved section, start at either the Beaver Creek Trailhead or the town of Vernonia. Starting in Tophill is also an option if you a willing to go 1 mile on gravel to reach the Vernonia paved section.

Attractions along the path include a fossil bed (called The Railroad Trestle Quarry) at the Tophill Trailhead (see map), two trestles over 600 feet high - one partially destroyed by a fire, and the pretty town of Vernonia. Due to safety concerns, the trestles are closed to any traffic and the path detours around them. The state park map issued for this trail is highly recommended. See Oregon State Parks under map resources at the end of this book.

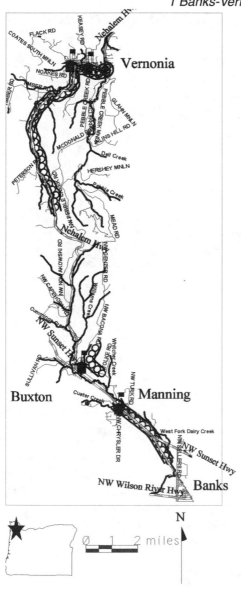

2 Forest Grove Hwy 47

Table 2-1. Path Data

Distance	City	County	End1	End2	Setting
2.2 mi.	Forest Grove	Washington	B St. & Tualatin Valley Hwy	Quince St. & Pacific Ave	Urban and rural

Table 2-2. Path Data

Path Surface
8 ft asphalt

The path starts out in the country

Getting There: Forest Grove is located 23 miles west of Portland on Highway 8.

In need of repair, this old path follows Tualatin Valley Highway in the southeast part of Forest Grove. It starts out in the country and ends in the east part of Forest Grove. It could serve as a commute path if you can stand the adjacent highway noise.

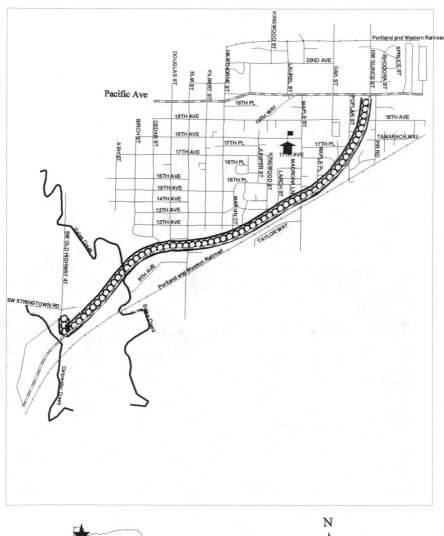

N

3 Brookwood

Table 3-1. Path Data

Distance	City	County	Map	Setting
6.0 mi.	Hillsboro	Washington	A	Park and business park

Table 3-2. Path Data

Path Surface
8 ft asphalt

Great path for a stroll

Getting There: Hillsboro is located 17 miles west of Portland. From Portland, take Highway 26 west and exit on Shute Road. Take Shute Road south for about a mile and a half and look for on-street parking.

http://www.PedalPals.com/

A lot of path mileage is packed into this space near the Hillsboro Airport. Made up of four loops and some spurs, this path snakes in and around the high-tech businesses scattered around Dawson Creek Park. Be cautious crossing the fairly busy but low speed streets.

4 Willow Creek Trail/Waterhouse Powerline Trail

Table 4-1. Path Data

Distance	City	County	Maps	Setting
1.8 mi.	Beaverton	Washington	A, D	Urban

Table 4-2. Path Data

Path Surface
8 ft asphalt

Table 4-3. Path Data

Internet
http://www.multnomah.lib.or.us/metro/parks/parks.html

http://www.PedalPals.com/

Taking the whole troop for a walk

Getting There: Exit southwest on NW Cornell Road from Highway 26 in Beaverton and go left (south) on NW 158th Avenue for a little less than half a mile.

Following Willow Creek going east to west and a powerline going north to south, this older path is situated in northwest Beaverton. A paved walking path that's too narrow for bikes makes up the east half of Willow Creek Trail.

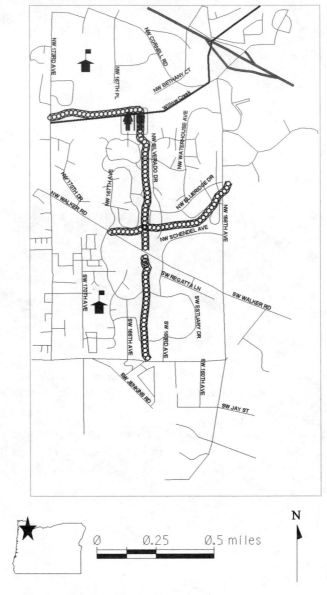

N

Ø   Ø.25   Ø.5 miles

5 Beaverton Powerline Trail, North

Table 5-1. Path Data

Distance	City	County	Maps	End1	End2
1.2 mi.	Beaverton	Washington	A, D	Burntwood St. near 158th Av.	Rigert Rd. near Rigert Ct.

Table 5-2. Path Data

Setting	Path Surface
Urban	8 ft asphalt

School kids out for a walk

5 Beaverton Powerline Trail, North

Getting There: In Beaverton, go west on Hart Road at the intersection of Hart Road and Murray Blvd. for three quarters of a mile.

A short neighborhood connector that goes along the Beaverton Powerline in the north-south portion and alongside Johnson Creek in the east-west part starting in Summercrest Park. This little path includes a tennis court and two play areas. Near the north end, close to Burntwood Street, the path becomes very steep. Otherwise, it's fairly flat.

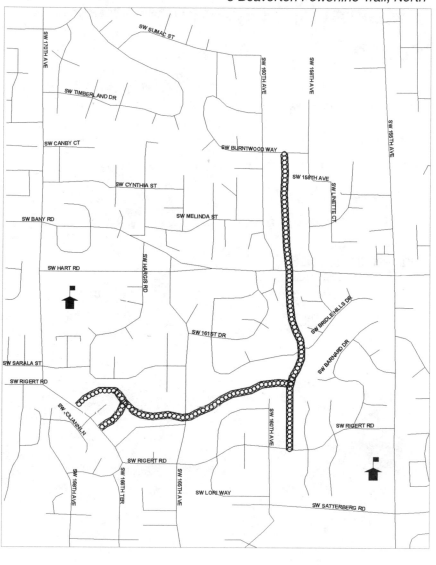

6 Murrayhill Powerline Park, South

Table 6-1. Path Data

Distance	City	County	Maps	End1	End2
1.8 mi.	Beaverton	Washington	A, D	Galena Way & SW 76th Ave	Old Schools Ferry Rd.

Table 6-2. Path Data

Setting	Path Surface
Urban	10 ft asphalt

Nice views on this part of the path

Getting There: In Beaverton, go west on Weir Road at the intersection of Weir Road and Murray Blvd. for three quarters of a mile or go southwest on Scholls Ferry Road one quarter of a mile past Murray Blvd.

This is a fairly hilly path that follows the Beaverton Powerline Greenway. It features a play area, tennis courts, and a small amphitheater. This path has many neighborhood connectors and some nice picnic opportunities.

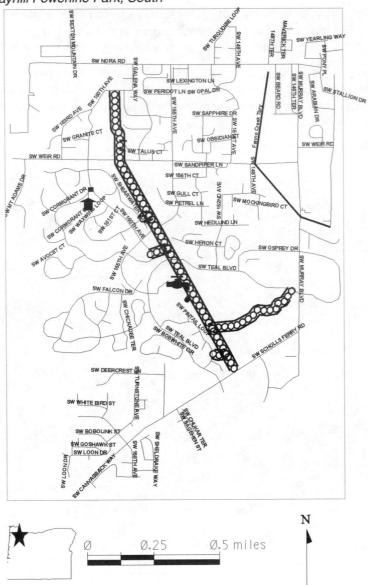

N

★

| Ø | Ø.25 | Ø.5 miles |

7 Fanno Creek Park, North

Table 7-1. Path Data

Distance	Cities	County	Maps	End1	End2
5.4 mi.	Beaverton, Tigard	Washington	A, D	Tigard St. near Tiedman St.	Denny St. near 111th St

Table 7-2. Path Data

Setting	Path Surface	Internet
Urban	8 ft asphalt	http://www.ci.beaverton.or.us/ http://www.thprd.com/

The historic Fanno Farmhouse

7 Fanno Creek Park, North

Getting There: You can access this path many places - one quarter of a mile west of Highway 217 on Denny Road or one mile west of Highway 217 on Hall Blvd, or one mile west of Highway 217 on Scholls Ferry Road.

Once part of Augustus Fanno's farm claim, this natural area of willows and ash is home to quite a bit of wildlife. The fairly high mileage greenway path that meanders through the claim has tons of playgrounds and as such might qualify as the most kid-frendly path. The only downside is the lack of a crossing at Hall Blvd. You need to walk to Greenway Street and Hall Blvd. to make the crossing. Hopefully, some day there will be an underpass so that you don't have to do this. Take a side trip and check out the New England-style Fanno Farmhouse.

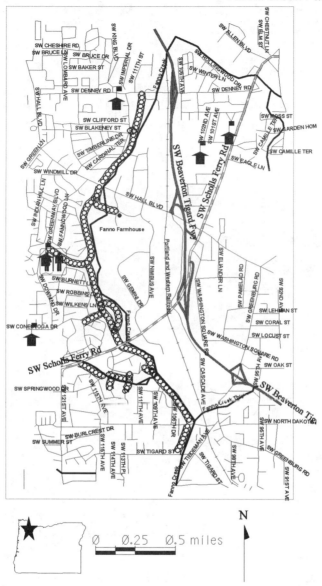

8 Fanno Creek Park, South

Table 8-1. Path Data

Distance	City	County	Map	End1	End2
1.1 mi.	Tigard	Washington	D	Main St near Johnson St.	Hall Blvd. near O'Mara St.

Table 8-2. Path Data

Setting	Path Surface	Internet
Urban	8 ft asphalt	*http://www.ci.beaverton.or.us/* *http://www.thprd.com/*

Near the Tigard City Hall

Getting There: In Tigard, go three quarters of a mile south of Highway 99 on Hall Blvd or go to Main Street near Johnson Street. Main Street parallels Highway 99 between Johnson Street and Greenburg Road.

This path mingles with Fanno Creek as it passes through Tigard. It's a good way to get to the library or city hall.

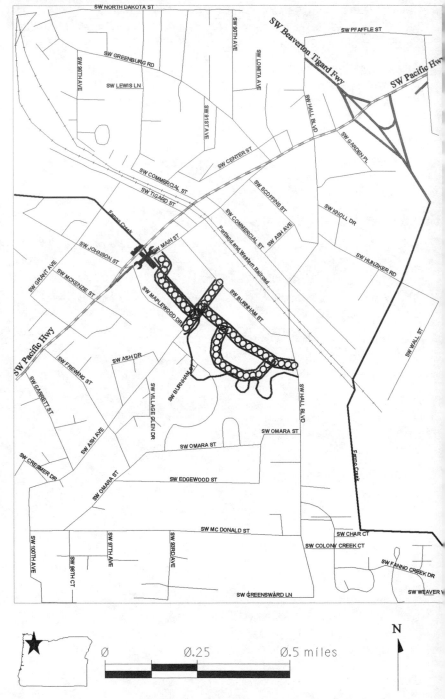

http://www.PedalPals.com/

9 Forest Glen Parkway

Table 9-1. Path Data

Distance	City	County	Maps	End1	End2
1.0 mi.	Beaverton	Washington	A, D	135th near Singletree Dr.	126th near SW Pioneer Ln.

Table 9-2. Path Data

Setting	Path Surface	Internet
Urban	8 ft asphalt	*http://www.thprd.org/*

Taking a car-free walk

Getting There: Go west from Highway 217 on Scholls Ferry Road for a

9 Forest Glen Parkway

little over one mile and then north on SW 125th for a block.

You might feel a bit walled in from all the cedar fences on this small stream-side path that winds through the neighborhoods of Beaverton.

http://www.PedalPals.com/

10 Summer Lake Park

Table 10-1. Path Data

Distance	City	County	Map	Setting	Path Surface
1.2 mi.	Tigard	Washington	D	Urban	8 ft asphalt, concrete

Table 10-2. Path Data

Internet
http://www.ci.tigard.or.us/

Walking the best friend

Getting There: Go west from Highway 217 on Scholls Ferry Road for one mile and a half then south on SW 130 Avenue for a quarter of a mile.

10 Summer Lake Park

This is a very scenic but short path around Summer Lake. Lovely back-yard gardens ring this park providing a beautiful touch to its ambiance.

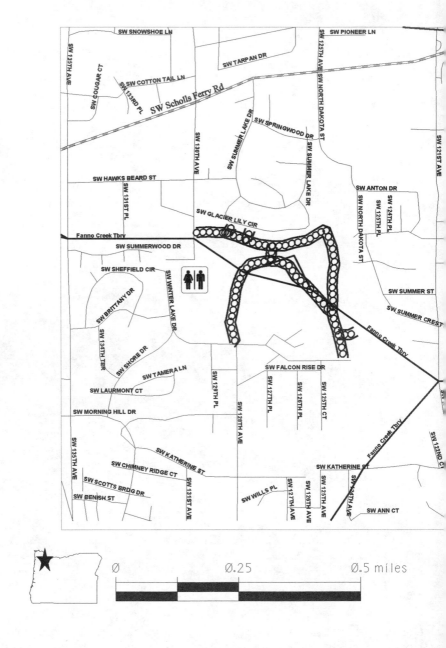

http://www.PedalPals.com/

11 Oregon Electric ROW Trail and Linear Park

Table 11-1. Path Data

Distance	City	County	End1	End2	Setting
1.2 mi.	Beaverton	Washington	Vista Brook Park	Oleson	Rail to Trail

Table 11-2. Path Data

Path Surface	Internet
8-11 ft asphalt	http://www.thprd.org/

Getting There: From Portland, take I-5 Exit #269B and head west on Multnomah Blvd for about 2 miles. Just after a sharp curve right, take a right turn on Oleson Road then an amost immediate left into the parking area for the Garden Home Recreation Center.

This path has a wide varicty of scenery for belng so short. Starting at the Recreation Center, it skirts the ball field, passes a very quaint woodland, and goes by a golf course where you will be protected from wayward golf balls by a very high fence. From here, it passes Vista Brook Park and ends at 92nd Avenue.

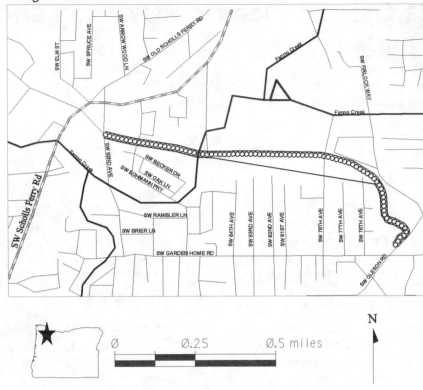

N

Ø   Ø.25   Ø.5 miles

12 Springwater Corridor

Table 12-1. Path Data

Distance	Cities	Counties	Maps	End1	End2
14.4 mi.	Portland, Gresham	Multinomah, Clackamas	A, B, C, E	near SE 28th Av. and SE Van Water St. Portland	Rugg Rd. and SE 267th Av.

Table 12-2. Path Data

Setting	Path Surface
Rail to Trail, urban and rural	10 ft sand seal, asphalt

Table 12-3. Path Data

Internet
http://www.parks.ci.portland.or.us/ Trails/SpringwaterCorridor/SWaterWelcome.htm http://www.portlandparks.org/Planning/SpringwaterOMSI.htm

One of the many bridges over Johnson Creek

Getting There: There are numerous path access points. The two main trailheads are at SE Johnson Creek Blvd. and SE 45th. in Portland or at SE Hogan Road in Gresham.

One of the longest paved paths in Oregon, this path shines as the classic rail-to-trail path. It is the major southeast segment of the 40 Mile Loop (see Marine Drive #1). Once the Springwater Division Railroad, it now serves as a prime example of how a path can serve commuters and recreational users to make a city more livable. More or less following the path of Johnson Creek, one of the last free-flowing streams in the Portland area, its scenery is extremely varied. From grimy industrial yards to wide open country with splendid views of Mt. Hood in the distance, you will see all this and more as you travel its length.

Starting from Portland, the first 13.3 miles of this path uses sand seal, an environmentally friendly surface that uses less oil than asphalt. You won't have any problems with this surface unless you are looking to set a new speed record. I wouldn't call it bumpy but it's just a tad wavy. Future plans call for extensions at both ends, west alongside an existing rail corridor to Oregon Museum of Science and Industry (OMSI) and east all the way to Estacada. Highlights along the path include the Tideman Johnson Nature Park, Bell Station (the last remaining Springwater train depot), Beggars-

Tick Wildlife Refuge, Powell Butte Park, Gresham Main City Park, and Columbia Brick Works, Oregon's oldest operating brick-works.

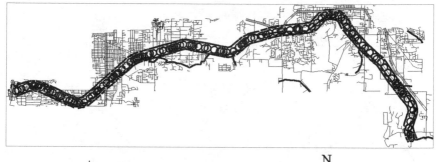

N

Ø   1   2   3   4 miles

13 I-205

Table 13-1. Path Data

Distance	City	Counties	Maps	End1	End2
16.0 mi.	Portland	Multinomah, Clackamas	A, B, E	SE 23rd St. Vancouver, WA	82nd & I-205

Table 13-2. Path Data

Setting	Path Surface
Urban	10 ft asphalt

Getting There: Almost any Exit from #13 to #27 on I-205.

This path is in very good shape and is one of the longest paved paths in Oregon. That's the good news. Ten to 15 percent of this path is behind sound barriers of concrete walls or dirt mounds. There are even a few places where you forget that you're right next to a very busy interstate. But this isn't enough to make up for the ear piercing sound of 65 mph traffic at point blank range. The absolute worst part, as far as maximum decibels, is the segment that runs right down the median of I-205 as it passes over the Columbia River. While this part is safe enough, there are concrete walls between you and the traffic, your ears are six feet from three lanes of the 65 mph deafening noise. I would strongly encourage ear plugs on this entire path and especially this Columbia River part. The highlight of this path is a one mile spur that heads west of Clark Road at I-205. It goes through a semi-wooded area along the Columbia Slough. This path can be used to commute to two malls, Clackamas Town Center near Sunnyside Road and I-205 or Mall 205 near Washington Street and I-205.

Inline skaters on the quiet side of the wall

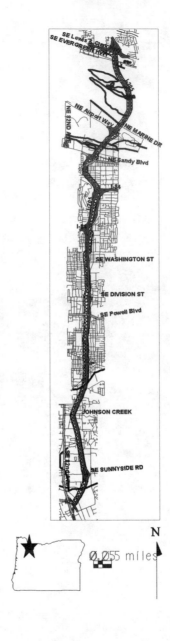

N

0.55 miles

http://www.PedalPals.com/

Table 14-1. Path Data

Distance	City	County	Maps	End1	End2	Setting
4.2 mi.	Portland	Multinomah	A, B, E	122nd Ave	207th	Urban

Table 14-2. Path Data

Path Surface	Internet
8 ft asphalt, 10 ft concrete	*http://www.parks.ci.portland.or.us/*

Not quite a car-free experience

Getting There: Take Exit #10 or #13 off of I-84 and immediately look for a place to park.

As if being right next to a freeway isn't enough, how about a concrete barrier to deflect the noise toward you? Ear plugs are mandatory.

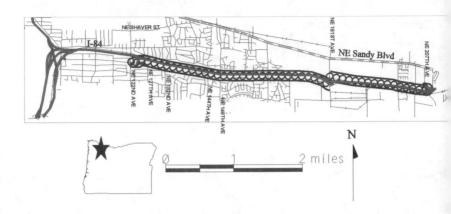

http://www.PedalPals.com/

15 Peninsula Crossing

Table 15-1. Path Data

Distance	City	County	Maps	End1
1.2 mi.	Portland	Multnomah	A, B	Willamette Blvd. & Ida Ave.

Table 15-2. Path Data

End2	Setting	Path Surface
Columbia Blvd. & N. Clarendon Ave.	Urban	8 - 12 ft asphalt

Table 15-3. Path Data

Internet
http://www.multnomah.lib.or.us/metro/parks/openspaces/segment1.html
http://www.metro-region.org/metro/parks/openspaces/peninsula.html
http://www.parks.ci.portland.or.us/

Near Fressenden Street.

Getting There: In Portland, take I-5 Columbia Blvd. Exit (#306A) and go west for about two and one half miles.

A rail link opened in 1908 between Portland and Vancouver, WA necessitated a large "cut" more than a mile long to maintain alignment between the Willamette River and the Columbia River. This cut consisted of more than 800,000 cubic yards of material and now makes up the railroad ravine next to this path. Starting at Ida Avenue and Willamette Blvd., the path is a widened sidewalk that crosses the start of the "cut" and then turns left to parallel it. It follows the deep gorge through neighborhoods as a narrow greenway until its end at Columbia Blvd.

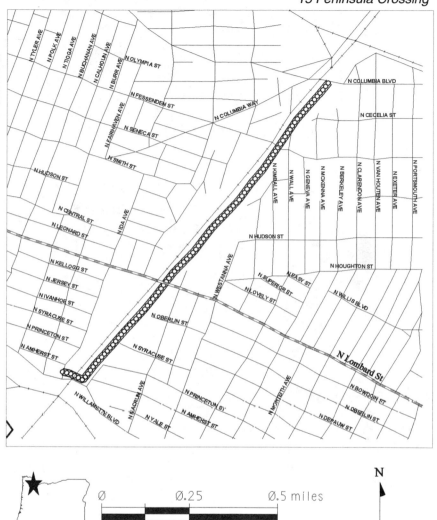

16 Marine Drive #1

Table 16-1. Path Data

Distance	City	County	Maps	End1	End2
3.8 mi.	Portland	Multinomah	A, B	1 mile west of Portland Rd on south side of Marine Dr	I-5 on Hayden Island near Jantzen Beach

Table 16-2. Path Data

Setting	Path Surface	Internet
Urban greenway	8-32 ft asphalt	http://www.parks.ci.portland.or.us/

The majestic Columbia River

Getting There: Exit #307 on I-5 and head west for about 2 miles on Marine Drive. Park in the Smith and Bybee Lakes Wildlife Area parking lot on the south side of Marine Drive.

Once connected, the Marine Drive paths will eventually make up part of a loop, that was coined "the 40 mile loop" by the Olmsted Brothers back in 1903. This loop, now 140 miles in length and connecting 30 parks, is completed only in pieces. These Marine Drive paths all go on or near the south bank of the Columbia River. They are at their best when they are immediately adjacent to the river and situated below the road where the noise level is very low (except when a jet passes overhead). The less scenic parts are amongst Portland's warehouses, airport and junkyards.

Beginning at a small parking area for the Smith and Bybee Lakes Wildlife Area (the largest wetlands inside an urban area in the U.S.), about 1 mile west of Portland Road and Marine Drive, the path is an old road that borders the wildlife area. It crosses Portland Road, turns left and heads toward the Columbia River. Along the river, it's raised above the road and provides good views of river traffic. This path does continue over I-5 to Vancouver, WA but it's only a 5 foot path so it's not covered in this book. When crossing the Columbia River on I-5, ear plugs are strongly recommended.

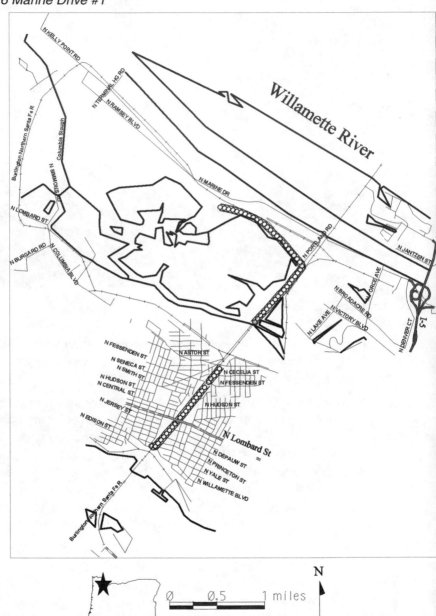

N

Ø____Ø.5____1 miles

http://www.PedalPals.com/

17 Marine Drive #2

Table 17-1. Path Data

Distance	City	County	Maps	End1	End2
5.0 mi.	Portland	Multinomah	A, B	33rd Dr. and Marine Dr	I-205 and Marine Dr

Table 17-2. Path Data

Setting	Path Surface	Internet
Urban greenway	10 - 12 ft asphalt	*http://www.parks.ci.portland.or.us/*

Near the Sea Scout Base and Portland Airport

17 Marine Drive #2

Getting There: Exit #307 on I-5 and head east for 2.5 miles on Marine Drive. Park on the gravel road just west of 33rd Drive off of Marine Drive.

See Marine Drive #1 for general information about Marine Drive paths. This path has a lot of scenic beauty but it's situated right next to Portland's airport (PDX) so be prepared for the occasional high decibel blasts of jet noise. From 33rd Drive, the path is on the city side of Marine Drive passing by the very end of the PDX runway until it crosses over Marine Drive at Broughton Park. It then descends below the road level and is next to the Columbia River where you get very nice views of river activity. Government Island then comes into view, you'll pass the Sea Scout Base and the path ends at I-205.

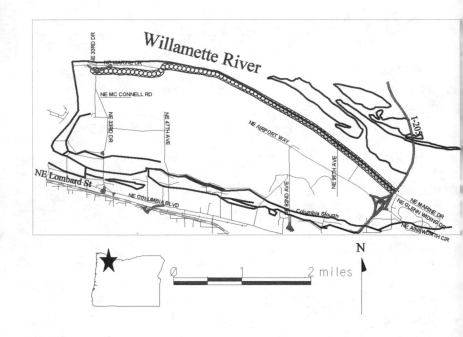

http://www.PedalPals.com/

18 Marine Drive #3

Table 18-1. Path Data

Distance	City	County	Maps	End1	End2
2.6 mi.	Portland	Multnomah	A, E	122nd Blvd	0.4 miles west of 185th St on Marine Drive

Table 18-2. Path Data

Setting	Path Surface	Internet
Urban greenway	8 ft asphalt	*http://www.parks.ci.portland.or.us/*

Getting There: Take Exit #24, Airport Way and head east for three quarters of a mile and then left (north) on 122nd. Park just before Marine Drive.

See Marine Drive #1 for general information about Marine Drive paths. This is perhaps the best of the Marine Drive paths, tons of nice river scenery with little airport noise. The path starts near 122nd and Marine (there is some parking on 122nd) where it follows a power line easement sandwiched between Marine Drive and the back of light industrial businesses on the city side of Marine Drive. You cross Marine Drive at 138th and now you're between the river and Marine Drive where it's very scenic. There is no parking at the end (End 2) located 0.4 miles west of Marine Drive and 185th.

In-line skating along the Columbia River

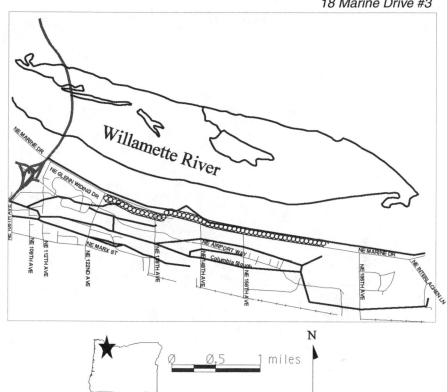

19 Marine Drive #4

Table 19-1. Path Data

Distance	Cities	County	Maps	End1	End2
2.6 mi.	Portland, Troutdale	Multinomah	A, E	Marine Dr. & Blue Lake Park Dr.	Troutdale Airport

Table 19-2. Path Data

Setting	Path Surface	Internet
Urban	8 ft asphalt	*http://www.parks.ci.portland.or.us/*

Getting There: Take Exit #14 on I-84 and go north on NE 207th Avenue for one half mile to NE Sandy Blvd. (Highway 30), turn right (east), go about one mile to Blue Lake Road (NE 223rd Avenue). Turn left (north) and go for a little more than a mile. You can park in Blue Lake Park for a nominal fee, or you can head east on Marine Drive and park on-street near the Troutdale Airport.

See Marine Drive #1 for general information about Marine Drive paths. This is my least favorite of the Marine Drive paths because most of it is far removed from the Columbia River. There is no parking at the west end (End 1) of this path unless you want to park in Blue Lake Park where it will cost you $3. You can park at the east end of the path on the shoulder of Marine Drive near the Troutdale Airport. This path is in need of some maintenance, tread slowly.

Out for a ride

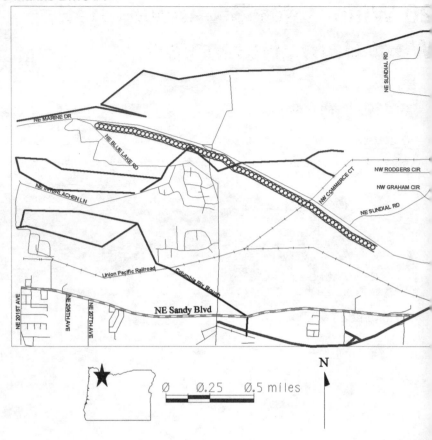

NE SUNDIAL RD

NE MARINE DR

NE BLUE LAKE RD

NW RODGERS CIR

NW GRAHAM CIR

NE INTERLACHEN LN

NW COMMERCE CT

NE SUNDIAL RD

Union Pacific Railroad

Columbia Riv Slough

NE Sandy Blvd

NE 201ST AVE

NE 205TH AVE

NE 207TH AVE

N

Ø   Ø.25   Ø.5 miles

http://www.PedalPals.com/

Table 20-1. Path Data

Distance	City	County	Maps	End1	End2
2.4 mi.	Portland	Multnomah	A, B	West bank under Broadway Bridge	Moody Ave under I-5 bridge

Table 20-2. Path Data

Setting	Path Surface
Urban	10 ft concrete

Table 20-3. Path Data

Internet
http://www.ci.portland.or.us/ http://www.multnomah.lib.or.us/metro/parks/parks.html

Jogging on the waterfront

Getting There: Parking can be difficult for this path but try Moody Avenue underneath I-5 as it passes over the west bank of the Willamette River. Heading north on I-5, Exit #299A and go east to Moody Avenue then proceed north until you are under I-5.

The ideal path for people watching, this part of the greenway passes by pedestrian shopping areas, lots of newly built riverfront townhouses and hotels, cruise boat docks, skyscrapers, and through riverfront parks. On nice days, this path swarms with walkers, cyclists, and inline skaters. It also passes the Saturday Market which runs on Saturday and Sunday under the Burnside Bridge. There are plans to extend this path both north and south.

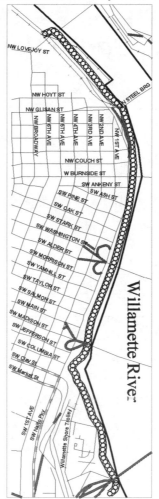

NW LOVEJOY ST

NW STEEL BRG

NW HOYT ST

NW GLISAN ST

NW BROADWAY
NW 6TH AVE
NW 4TH AVE
NW 3RD AVE
NW 2ND AVE
NW 1ST AVE

NW COUCH ST

W BURNSIDE ST

SW ANKENY ST

SW ASH ST

SW PINE ST

SW OAK ST

SW STARK ST

SW WASHINGTON ST

SW ALDER ST

SW MORRISON ST

SW YAMHILL ST

SW TAYLOR ST

SW SALMON ST

SW MAIN ST

SW MADISON ST

SW JEFFERSON ST

SW COLUMBIA ST

SW CLAY ST

SW Market St

Willamette River

SW 1ST AVE
SW Naito Pkwy

Willamette Shore Trolley

N

Ø   Ø.25   Ø.5 miles

21 Willamette Greenway Trail, West Bank, South Part

Table 21-1. Path Data

Distance	City	County	Maps	End1	End2
3.0 mi.	Portland	Multinomah	A, B	Near the Ross Island Bridge	Tacoma St. north of Sellwood Bridge

Table 21-2. Path Data

Setting	Path Surface
Urban	8 ft asphalt concrete

Table 21-3. Path Data

Internet
http://www.ci.portland.or.us/ *http://www.multnomah.lib.or.us/metro/parks/parks.html*

The path in Willamette Park

Getting There: Take I-5 Exit #297 and go south on SW Terwilliger Blvd. for about one half mile, then turn left (east) on SW Taylors Ferry Road. Go for about one mile and turn right (south) on SW Macadam Avenue. Go for one half of a mile to just south of the Macadam Bay Club to the boat ramp and park.

This path starts at the Macadam Bay Club but there is no parking here. Park just south of the Club at the boat ramp. Beginning as a 4 foot (!) wide path along the busy Macadam Avenue, it quickly widens to 8 feet and winds through a small dilapidated neighborhood and then into Willamette Park. There you can access the Willamette Shore Trolley which runs from downtown Portland to Lake Oswego. At this point, you are across the Willamette River from Oaks Amusement Park where, on weekends, you will hear amusement ride sounds drifting across the river. From this park, the path heads north along the river through an industrial area then turns into a widened sidewalk on Riverside Lane.

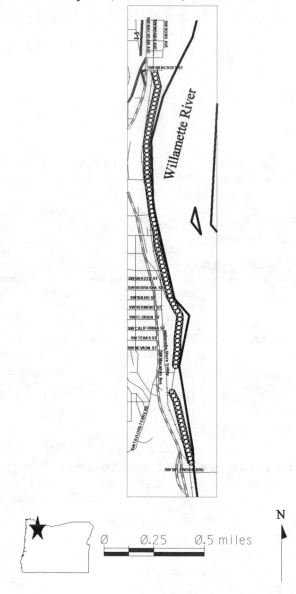

N

Ø   Ø.25   Ø.5 miles

22 Willamette River, East Bank

Table 22-1. Path Data

Distance	City	County	Map	End1	End2
1.8 mi.	Portland	Multinomah	A	East bank & Steel Bridge	West end of Caruthers St.

Table 22-2. Path Data

Setting	Path Surface
Urban	10 ft concrete

Table 22-3. Path Data

Internet
http://www.ci.portland.or.us/
http://www.multnomah.lib.or.us/metro/parks/parks.html

The floating section of the path

Getting There: A good place to start is in the OMSI parking lot. Take I-5 Exit #300 and follow the signs to OMSI.

Just completed, this path sports nicely manicured landscaping and cute street signs. Sandwiched between I-5 and the Willamette River, it has a section that floats right on the river. It's also a good path to combine with a visit to OMSI. It's pretty noisy in spots due to its proximity to I-5.

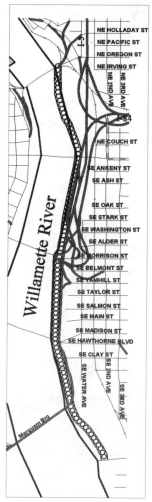

N

Ø	Ø.25	Ø.5 miles

23 Kruse Way

Table 23-1. Path Data

Distance	City	County	End1	End2	Setting
1.2 mi.	Lake Oswego	Clackamas	Boones Ferry Rd.	Kruse Oaks Dr.	Urban

Table 23-2. Path Data

Path Surface
8 ft asphalt

Perfect landscaping

Getting There: Take I-5 Exit #292 and go east on Kruse Way for one quarter mile and park on or near Kruse Oaks Drive.

http://www.PedalPals.com/

This bumpy path has pretty landscape as it passes apartments and small businesses.

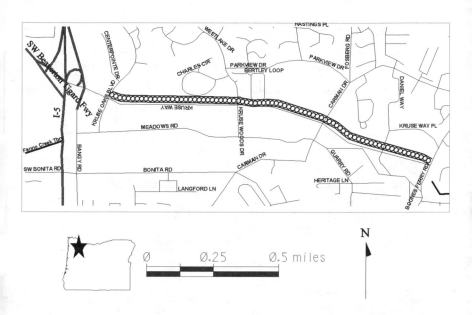

24 Tryon Creek State Park

Table 24-1. Path Data

Distance	City	Counties	Cost	Maps	Setting
2.7 mi.	Lake Oswego	Multnomah, Clackamas	state park entrance fee	A, U	Park

Table 24-2. Path Data

Path Surface	Internet
8 ft asphalt	*http://www.oregonstateparks.org*

No shortage of greenery on this path

http://www.PedalPals.com/

Getting There: Take I-5 Exit #297 and go south on SW Terwilliger Blvd. for about one and one quarter miles to Boones Ferry Road and find parking near here. Or continue another mile to the state park entrance where an entrance fee or park sticker is required. You could also park near the intersection of SW Terwilliger Blvd. and SW Riverside Drive near Lake Oswego.

Imagine a paved path through lush jungle-like rain forest in the middle of metro Portland. Tryon Creek is probably as close as you'll come to it. Starting from its most northern point, this path descends on a slight grade all the way to Lake Oswego. Halfway down the path is a nature center with educational exhibits and programs. The northern 1/4 of the path is old but in pretty good shape, the middle 1/3 is brand new and the southern part is in pretty bad shape and should not be ridden at high speed.

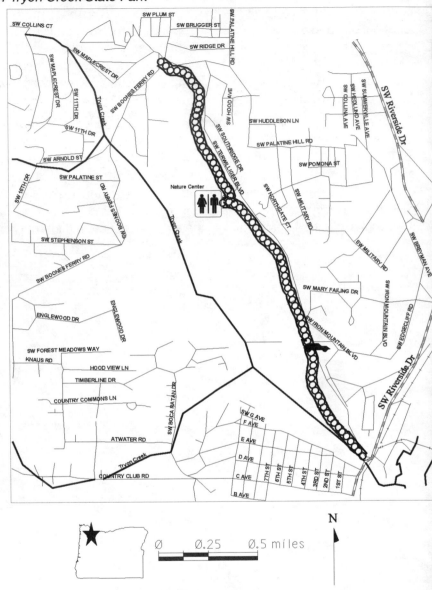

Nature Center

Tryon Creek

N

0   0.25   0.5 miles

http://www.PedalPals.com/

25 Tualatin River Greenway, Cook Park

Table 25-1. Path Data

Distance	City	County	Map	End1	End2
1.4 mi.	Tigard	Washington	D	108th Ave near Tualatin Riverwood Ln	Cook Park

Table 25-2. Path Data

Setting	Path Surface
Park	8 ft asphalt, some 5 ft

Table 25-3. Path Data

Internet
http://www.ci.tigard.or.us/PARKS/cook1.htm

In Cook Park

Getting There: Take I-5 Exit #291 and head west on Upper Boones Ferry Road for about one half mile, then turn right (west) on Durham Road and go about one mile and turn left (south) on SW 92nd Avenue. Park at the end.

This is a short path that goes between the north shore of the Tualatin River and adjacent neighborhoods ending at Cook Park. The west end of this path starts out very steep; the rest is fairly flat.

26 Faraday Lane

Table 26-1. Path Data

Distance	City	County	End1	End2
3.9 mi.	Estacada	Clackamas	South of Estacada	North Fork Reservoir

Table 26-2. Path Data

Setting	Path Surface
Rural, Clackamas River	30 ft asphalt

The Clackamas River and the end of the 1.9 mile fish ladder

Getting There: From I-205, take Exit #12 east (OR 224). Follow OR 224 for about 20 miles to Estacada. Continue on OR 224 for 1.5 miles south east of Estacada and turn right on Faraday Lane. Park in the Portland General Electric parking area. If you are coming north on I-5, take exi

#271 and follow the signs to Molalla. Continue on OR 211 to OR 224 then turn right (south) for 1 mile. Park in the Portland General Electric parking area. To get to the south end of the path (End2), go on OR 224 for 5.7 miles southeast of Estacada (near mile marker 29) and turn at the sign "Faraday Rd. N. Fork Reservoir". Park in the gravel lot by the reservoir.

Strictly speaking, this is not a path but a Portland General Electric service drive so be aware that you may see a rare PGE truck on this road. After severe flooding in 1996, this section of what was Oregon 224 was closed off except for non-motorized use and PGE trucks. Starting at the PGE parking area, you need to go 0.5 miles to the gate. This portion of the road is used by the public. After the gate, the road parallels the Clackamas River and provides beautiful views of the whitewater down below through the trees. Next you will see the Faraday Diversion Dam where a 1.9 mile long fish ladder, one of the longest in the world, ends. The road continues along the Reservoir and ends at the south gate. This path might be too difficult for small children as its length and gentle grade combine for a somewhat strenuous ride when going south. Northbound is all downhill. This path is only open during daylight hours.

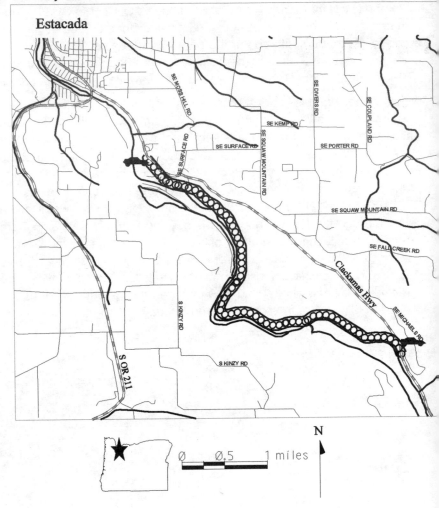

Estacada

N

Ø   Ø.5   1 miles

http://www.PedalPals.com/

27 Columbia River Waterfront Trail/Tidewater Cove Trail

Table 27-1. Path Data

Distance	Cities	County	Map	End1	End2
4.3 mi.	Vancouver, WA	Clark	G	Columbia Way south of 3rd St.	Wintler Park

Table 27-2. Path Data

Setting	Path Surface
River Greenway	14 ft concrete, 8 ft concrete sidewalk

Table 27-3. Path Data

Internet
http://www.ci.vancouver.wa.us/parks-recreation/trails.htm

Near Fort Vancouver National Park

Getting There: Take I-5 into Vancouver and take exit #1B. Turn Left onto E 6th Street. Take 6th Street towards the city center and continue on W 6th Street. Turn Left on West Columbia Street and go under I-5 and find the closest parking. The path starts just east of where West Columbia Way goes underneath I-5. Parking is also available in Wintler Park.

When this path is near the river it's wonderful, with its broad river vistas and pretty natural areas viewed from benches, grassy patches, or viewing platforms.

Starting at I-5 on a widened sidewalk on the river side of Columbia Way, it runs along the river passing the Captain Vancouver Monument, honoring the British captain who explored the Pacific Coast in 1792. To the left will be a side path to Old Apple Tree Park which has the oldest apple tree in the area. Later, in front of some townhouses, you will pass the statue of Ilchee (Moon Girl), honoring the region's early native inhabitants through the likeness of a Chinook noblewoman. Just before the path seems to end, you'll need to skirt left on a narrow path between two restaurants and then angle to the right through an apartment parking lot to Columbia River Way. On Columbia River Way, proceed down the widened sidewalk for a little over a mile to the entrance to Marine Park. This section of the path has many business driveway conflicts so be careful through here. Near the entrance to Marine Park is the Henry J. Kaiser Shipyard Memorial which has an interpretive center and great views from its three-story viewing tower. Inside Marine Park, you will find restrooms, play areas, benches, picnic shelters, and the Water Resources Education Center. WREC's charter is to teach people of all ages to make wise decisions about water and the environment it supports. It has a 350-gallon aquarium, water sciences lab, a computer game room, and an exhibit hall. Hours are 9am to 5pm Monday through Saturday and 9am to 8pm Thursday. Admission is free; call (360) 696-8478 for more information. After Marine Park, the path goes along the shore of the Columbia River. It then goes around some private property to enter Wintler Park where it ends. Parking is available here.

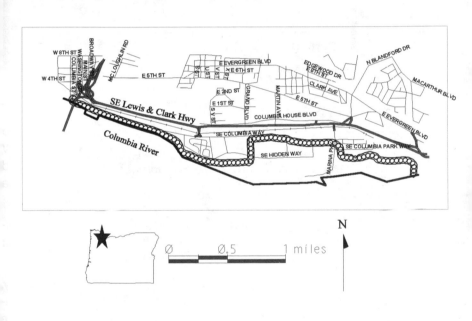

28 Salmon Creek Greenway Trail

Table 28-1. Path Data

Distance	Cities	County	Map	End1	End2
3.9 mi.	Vancouver, WA	Clark	G	117th Street near I-5	NW 36th Avenue near Creekside Drive

Table 28-2. Path Data

Setting	Path Surface
Creek Greenway	8-11 ft asphalt

Table 28-3. Path Data

Internet
http://www.ci.vancouver.wa.us/parks-recreation/trails.htm

Fishing at Klineline Pond

Getting There: Take I-5 into Vancouver, take Exit #5 (99th Street) then go west on NE 99th Street for one third mile. Then turn right (north) on Hazel Dell Avenue and go about one and a half miles to the Salmon Creek Greenway Park parking lot.

Starting in Salmon Creek Greenway Park, this path winds around Klineline Pond and then heads along the very scenic Salmon Creek. As the path moves away from the park, it enters a wide canyon-like grassy area. As the creek widens, the path sticks to the south shore somewhat above the flood plain and goes through a very pretty grove. This path is slightly hilly but is still recommended for small children.

N

http://www.PedalPals.com/

29 Discovery Trail West

Table 29-1. Path Data

Distance	Cities	County	Map	End1	End2
1.5 mi.	Vancouver, WA	Clark	G	NW Fruit Valley Road & Bernie Drive	Hazel Dell Avenue near Alki Road

Table 29-2. Path Data

Setting	Path Surface
Creek Greenway	8-11 ft asphalt

Table 29-3. Path Data

Internet
http://www.ci.vancouver.wa.us/parks-recreation/trails.htm

A shady part of the path

Getting There: Take I-5 into Vancouver, exit Hazel Dell Avenue and take it north. Park on Alki Road.

Passing through a beautiful wooded area, this path follows Burnt Bridge Creek and ends when the creek turns into a reservoir. This path and Discovery Trail East will be linked soon.

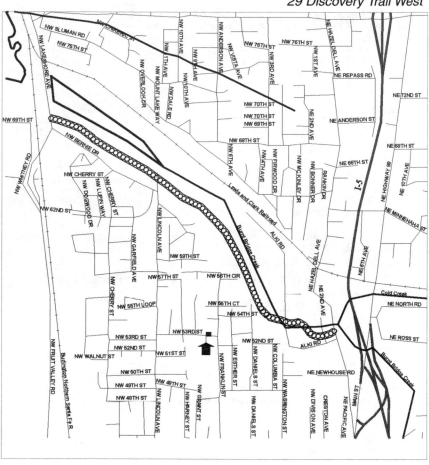

30 Discovery Trail East

Table 30-1. Path Data

Distance	Cities	County	Map	End1	End2
1.3 mi.	Vancouver, WA	Clark	G	Arnold Park	End of Nicholson Road west of Falk Road

Table 30-2. Path Data

Setting	Path Surface
Creek Greenway	8-11 ft asphalt

Table 30-3. Path Data

Internet
http://www.ci.vancouver.wa.us/parks-recreation/trails.htm

Getting There: Take I-5 into Vancouver, take Exit #2 (39th Street) then go east on West 39th Street then left (north) on 15th Street. Then go right (east) on NE 41st Street Circle and park at the end of the street.

This fairly hilly (but okay for small children) little path goes mainly through Arnold Park. It makes an unmarked jog at St. Johns Blvd, be sure to cross at the light here. This path and Discovery Trail West will be linked soon.

Bridge over Burnt Bridge Creek

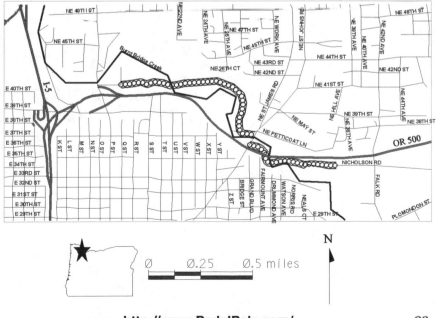

Part 2. Oregon Coast

These paths along the beautiful Oregon coast are unique in that they allow you easy access to the beach and estuaries of the Oregon coast.

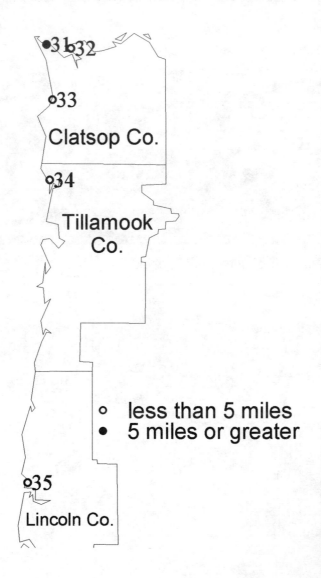

●31 ●32

○33

Clatsop Co.

○34

Tillamook Co.

○   less than 5 miles
●   5 miles or greater

○35

Lincoln Co.

31 Ft. Stevens State Park

Table 31-1. Path Data

Distance	City	County	Cost	Map	Setting
8.3 mi.	Hammond	Clatsop	state park entrance fee	U	Park

Table 31-2. Path Data

Path Surface	Internet
8 feet Asphalt	*http://www.oregonstateparks.org*

The 40 and 8 Boxcar, a gift from France

31 Ft. Stevens State Park

Getting There: The historic area of Ft. Stevens State Park is located where the Columbia River meets the Pacific Ocean. It is west of the town of Hammond, approximately 10 miles from Astoria. From Astoria proceed west through Warrenton to Hammond. At the stoplight in Hammond, go straight and then turn right into the Old Ft Stevens Civil War Earthworks and Museum area. Astoria, in the northwest corner of Oregon, can be reached from Portland via U.S. 30 following the Columbia River westward or Hwy 26 to Seaside. From Seaside, proceed north on U.S. 101 along the coast turning left at the Ft. Stevens turn off (well marked) and follow the signs to the park. There is no fee if you ride your bike into the park from Hammond (see map). Note that there is a gate on the path going to Hammond that is locked from 4pm to 10am.

Not many bike paths will get you to a shipwreck but at Ft. Stevens, originally built during the Civil War to protect the mouth of the Columbia River you can pedal to the wreck of the *Peter Iredale*. One of the most photographed shipwrecks in the world, this English sailing ship ran aground in 1906 amidst a strong southwest wind and soup-like fog. This path is comprised mostly of a loop in the southern half of the park. The path goes through some very pretty sections of coastal pines made up of western hemlock and Sitka spruce among others. A spur off of the main loop leads right to the beach and to the Iredale, its huge skeletal remains sticking out of the sand. For the most part, this path passes through the beautiful nature areas of the park and doesn't mingle with the historical sections of the park. It does pass near Battery Russell, the target of a 10 minute Japanese sub attack in 1942, the only attack to ever be waged on the Fort.

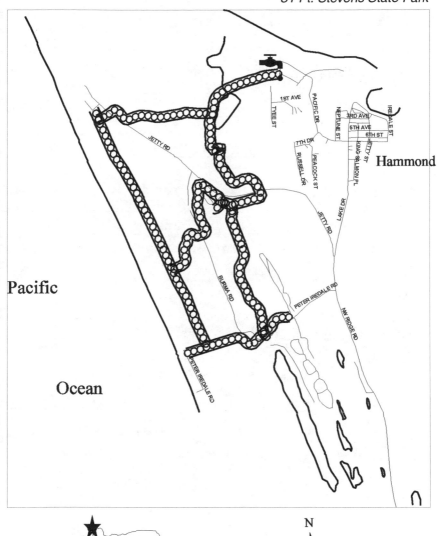

Pacific

Ocean

Hammond

N

Ø   0.25   0.5 miles

32 Astoria Riverwalk

Table 32-1. Path Data

Distance	City	County	End1	End2	Setting
1.9 mi.	Astoria	Clatsop	6th St.	39th St.	Rail to Trail

Table 32-2. Path Data

Path Surface	Internet
11 ft wood, asphalt	*http://www.astoria-usa.com/*

The historic Astoria Riverfront Trolley

Getting There: Astoria is located on Highway 30, 95 miles northwest of Portland. If you're coming from the coast just take Highway 101 north and when you enter Astoria take Highway 30 east. A good place to park is in the Columbia River Maritime Museum parking lot near the corner of 17th Street and Highway 30. The Maritime Museum itself is definitely

http://www.PedalPals.com/

worth a visit.

Beginning as a wooden plank path, this path later runs adjacent to a 40 passenger tourist trolley line that's totally run by volunteers. The wooden part of the path passes many fisheries and restaurants and runs to 9th Street, where it turns into a wide sidewalk for a few blocks, passes the Maritime Museum, and then runs until 39th Street. Ultimately it will be five miles long and end at Tongue Point. The entire path runs right along the Columbia River. Astoria is the first permanent European-American settlement west of the Mississippi River, established as Fort Astoria in 1811. This is an especially fun day trip for the family. You can complement your bike ride with a visit to the Columbia River Marine Museum, a trolley ride, and lunch at one of the many riverside restaurants.

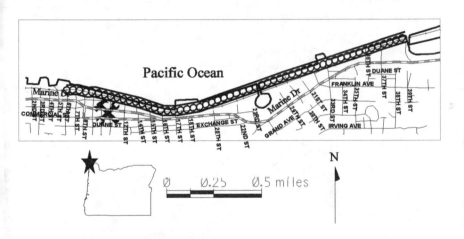

33 Seaside Promenade

Table 33-1. Path Data

Distance	City	County	End1	End2	Setting
1.5 mi.	Seaside	Clatsop	Avenue U	12th Avenue	Beach Promenade

Table 33-2. Path Data

Path Surface	Internet
14 ft concrete	*http://www.clatsop.com/seaside*

A fun ride in a surrey

Getting There: Seaside is 79 miles from Portland on the Oregon coast. From Portland, take Highway 26 west 75 miles to Highway 101 then 4 miles north to Seaside. Parking can be a problem during the busy summer months so try to avoid the area near Broadway Drive and the Promenade. Instead, head west at the intersection of Avenue U and Highway 101 and park near Avenue U and Beach Drive. If you're coming from the north, go west at the intersection of 12th Avenue and Highway 101 and go as far as you can on 12th Avenue.

This popular beach resort town, the oldest one on the Pacific Northwest coast, offers a 14 foot wide classic oceanfront promenade, known locally as "The Prom". It features a wide sandy beach leading to the Pacific Ocean with easy access on one side and lovely old homes mixed with a few motels and condos on the other side. Sights along the "Prom" include a 60 year old aquarium and the Lewis and Clark Salt Works where the expedition spent the winter of 1805 boiling sea water to make salt for their return trip. The "Prom", built in 1920, can become very busy with pedestrian traffic in the height of the tourist season so be careful.

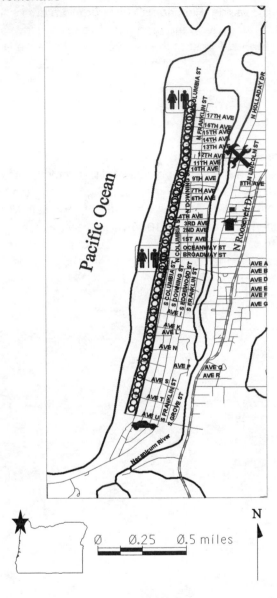

http://www.PedalPals.com/

34 Nehalem Bay State Park

Table 34-1. Path Data

Distance	City	County	Cost	Map	Setting
1.5 mi.	Manzanita	Tillamook	state park entrance fee	U	Park

Table 34-2. Path Data

Path Surface	Internet
8 ft asphalt	*http://www.oregonstateparks.org*

A four-legged park resident about to cross the path

Getting There: Nehalem Bay State Park is located just south of Manzanita on the Oregon coast. From Portland, take Highway 26 west to the coast and then head south on Highway 101 or take Highway 26 west to Highway 6 then west to Highway 101 then north to Manzanita. Then follow signs a mile to Nehalem Bay State Park's entrance.

This cute little path, which encircles a small airstrip, is nestled in a sand spit between the Nehalem River and the Pacific Ocean. This spit was once home to a Salish salmon fishing camp from 1300-1600. The path used to be longer but a small chunk was lost due to shore erosion near the south end of the airstrip's paved runway. Be careful when crossing the street as the posted speed limit of 40 MPH is absurd.

If you go clear out to the end of the spit, you will see hundreds of harbor seals. But don't get too close to them! They are easily disturbed and that can cause them to expend valuable energy or even roll over and crush their young. It is illegal to harass them. Just take your binoculars and look from the dunes.

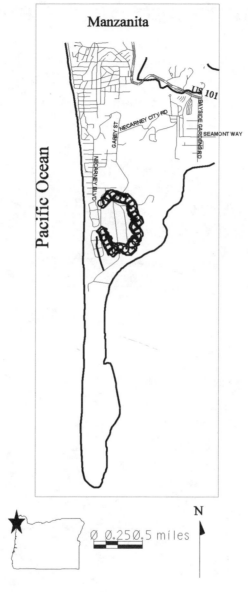

35 South Beach State Park

Table 35-1. Path Data

Distance	City	County	Cost	Map	Setting
1.1 mi.	Newport	Lincoln	state park entrance fee	U	Park

Table 35-2. Path Data

Path Surface	Internet
10 ft asphalt	*http://www.oregonstateparks.org*

A foggy ride near the beach

Getting There: Go to the coast and take Highway 101 two and a half miles south of Newport and look for signs to South Beach State Park.

This path connects the South Jetty with the Day-Use Area of the park. Once a wetland, this area was hand planted years ago and now is made up of beach grass and some red huckleberries.

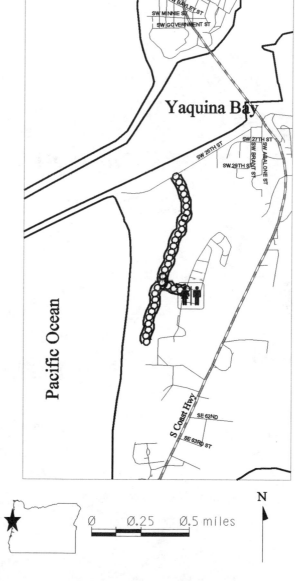

Part 3. Mid Willamette Valley

These path encompass the Mid Willamette Valley area, including Salem, Corvallis, and Albany.

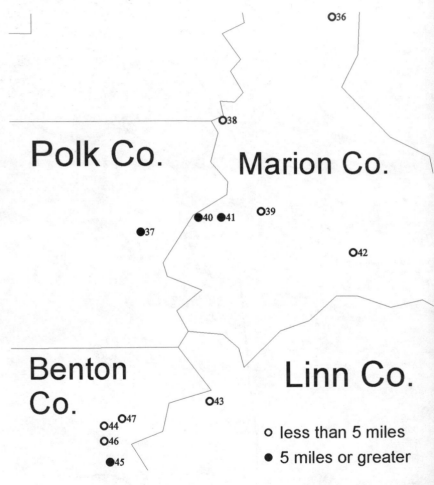

36 Champoeg State Park

Table 36-1. Path Data

Distance	City	County	Cost	Maps	Setting
3.2 mi.	Butteville	Marion	state park entrance fee	H, U	Park

Table 36-2. Path Data

Path Surface	Internet
8 ft asphalt	http://www.oregonstateparks.org

A feathered friend along the path

Getting There: From Portland, take I-5 Exit #282 (Miley Road) and go west (it turns into Butteville Road) for about 4 miles and park in Butteville. Ride your bike south on Butteville Road for one quarter of a mile and turn right on Schuler Road. Alternately, follow the signs to Champoeg State Park and pay the admission fee or have a state park sticker. Coming from the south, take I-5 Exit #278 and follow Ehlen Road west for about 2 miles to Butteville Road. Then go north to Butteville or follow the signs to the state park entrance.

Bearing a name that is Native American in origin and pronounced "Sham pooie", Champoeg is recognized in the minds of many as the birthplace of Oregon. Although strictly speaking, it is not. Once home to the Kala puya Indians, it had the Pacific Coast's first provisional American govern ment. This was one of the principal factors which led to Oregon becoming a United States Territory in 1848 and ultimately, to becoming the Union's 33rd state in 1859.

There is a visitor's center located to the right of the entry road to the park. Here one finds the Newellsville Museum Store which has various items for sale, books about the life and times of the early settlers, trinkets, old fashioned stick candy, beef jerky, etc. On display in the museum portion of the building are a number of items left from a bygone era and an auditorium where meetings are often held.

The park has scenic views of the Willamette River, camping and picnic facilities. The path starts by the Riverside Day Use Area and goes al most all the way to Butteville. It's nicely shaded and passes some histori sites (Pioneer Mothers Cabin Museum, First Newell House, and Manson House), the group picnic area, the campground, and a very scenic por tion of the Willamette River. You will pass areas where Native American women used to dig large quantities of the roots which they called pooitch every fall. Some portions of the path need some maintenance so don go too fast.

Butteville

NE WILSONVILLE RD

NE EARLWOOD RD

SCHULER RD NE

Willamette River

Willamette River

CHAMPOEG RD NE

CHAMPOEG RD NE

BUTTEVILLE RD NE

Mission Court

N

0   0.5   1 miles

37 Rickreall to Monmouth

Table 37-1. Path Data

Distance	Cities	County	Map	End1	End2
5.5 mi.	Rickreall, Monmouth	Polk	H	Rickreall	Monmouth

Table 37-2. Path Data

Setting	Path Surface
Adjacent busy 2 lane road	8 ft asphalt

Entering Monmouth

Getting There: Take Highway 22 west of Salem for about 10 miles and then south on Highway 99W to Rickreall. From Eugene, take Highway 99W north about 60 miles to Monmouth.

Running close to busy Highway 99W between Rickreall and Monmouth

http://www.PedalPals.com/

this older path is a bit worn and noisy but provides a way to get from one small town to another. More towns need this kind of connection but hopefully not right next to a busy highway.

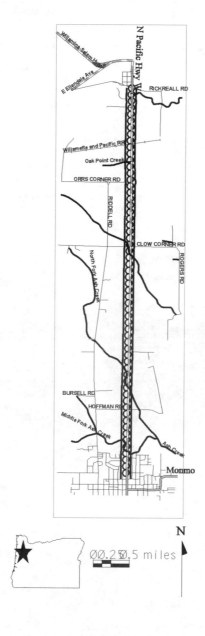

38 Willamette Mission State Park

Table 38-1. Path Data

Distance	City	County	Cost	Maps	Setting
3.9 mi.	Keizer	Marion	state park entrance fee	H, U	Park

Table 38-2. Path Data

Path Surface	Internet
8 ft asphalt	*http://www.oregonstateparks.org*

Plenty of blackberries along this path

Getting There: Willamette Mission State Park is located about 10 miles north of Keizer on Wheatland Road. You can park for free on the west bank of the Willamette River at the Wheatland Ferry docks. Parking on the east terminus (state park side) requires a state park sticker or daily fee. The west terminus (Wheatland) can be reached by going on Highway 99W to Amity and then east on Amity Road 12 miles to Highway 221. Then south on 221 for half a mile, then west on Wheatland Road to the ferry. Leave your car in the ferry parking lot (it's free). Take your bike on the ferry crossing the Willamette River to the other side. The ferry is free for bicycles and pedestrians. When on the other side, you can easily find the path by going south and looking for a small bridge over a creek.

Alternatively, you can follow the signs to the park entrance and either pay the daily admission or have a yearly sticker.

Very similar to Champoeg, this park is in a lowland along the Willamette River in amongst blackberry bushes, filbert groves, and the state's biggest black cottonwood tree. The path provides you with very nice views of the Willamette River and the open lowlands that occupy the area and provide many picnic opportunities. Many families with small children do one or two segments of the total path. And don't miss the free ferry ride!

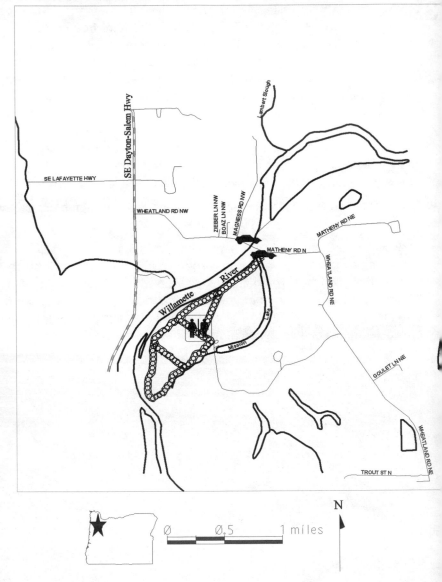

http://www.PedalPals.com/

39 Salem Parkway

Table 39-1. Path Data

Distance	City	County	Map	End1	End2
2.6 mi.	Salem	Marion	H	Chemawa Rd. and Salem Parkway	Cherry Ave. and Salem Parkway

Table 39-2. Path Data

Setting	Path Surface
Urban	10 ft asphalt

Not much between you and the highway

Getting There: Take I-5 Exit #260, head west and park nearby.

39 Salem Parkway

Running alongside the Salem Parkway, a main artery connecting Salem with Portland bound I-5, this path won't win any awards for aesthetics. The deafening noise will deter many. Having a limited potential as a commute path to downtown, it's probably used more by children to get from nearby neighborhoods to Kennedy Elementary School.

http://www.PedalPals.com/

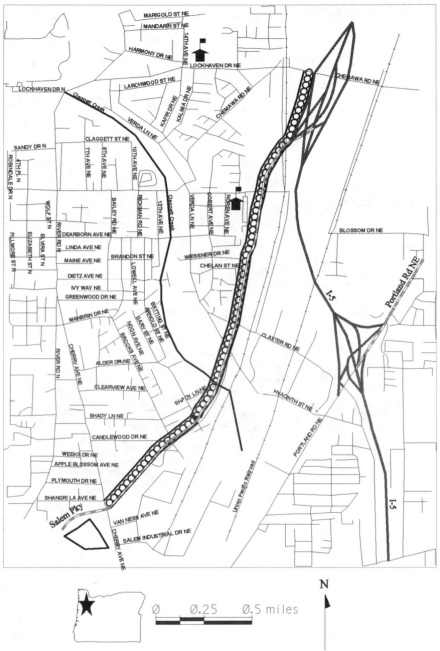

40 Salem Hwy 22

Table 40-1. Path Data

Distance	City	County	Map	End1	End2
5.3 mi.	Salem	Polk	H	Edgewater St. & Eola Dr.	Hwy 22 & Rickreall Rd.

Table 40-2. Path Data

Setting	Path Surface
City, Rural	8 ft asphalt

Going through Holman State Wayside

Getting There: From the east, head to downtown Salem and go across the Willamette River on Marion Street. Then follow Highway 22 for a little over one mile and park near Eola Drive. From the west, go east on Highway 22 from Rickreall (on Highway 99W) for about three miles to

http://www.PedalPals.com/

Rickreall Road. Park on Rickreall Road.

This is a path that won't win any awards for aesthetics. This path was built in the early 1970's and is one of the very early ones in the state. It's basically an eight foot wide sidewalk alongside the busy Highway 22 westbound out of Salem on its way to Dallas. Barely off-street and crossing way too many driveways and business accesses, this is a good example of how not to build a multi-use path. The high points of this path are when it goes through Holman State Wayside with its shady picnic area and views of the Coastal Range to the west. Further west after it crosses Highway 22 on a bike bridge, there is a memorial to Ricky Allan who served on the Oregon Bicycle Advisory Committee. He served as the youngest member of the committee and subsequently died in an Air Force plane crash. If you continue on Rickreall Road. (on street) this trip can be combined with the Rickreall to Monmouth path for a ride from Salem to Monmouth for a total of about 14 miles each way.

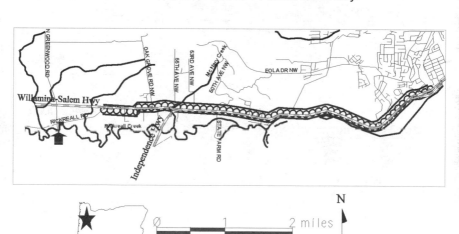

41 Minto-Brown Island Park

Table 41-1. Path Data

Distance	City	County	Map	End1	End2
8.9 mi.	Salem	Marion	H	Miller St. & River Rd.	Faragate Ave. & Homestead Rd.

Table 41-2. Path Data

Setting	Path Surface
Park, River	8 ft asphalt

Table 41-3. Path Data

Internet
http://www.salemhomeplace.com/ pages/community/pages/parks/mintobrown.html

Scooters work fine on this path

Getting There: From downtown Salem, take Commercial Street south about one mile and a half and turn right (west) on Owens Street. Continue on Owens Street for about a mile and turn right (north) at Homestead Road (at a light), go across the railroad tracks and into the park. Turn right into the parking lot. There is access to the path at the end of the parking lot.

Situated in a south neighborhood in Salem, this path starts as a widened sidewalk alongside River Road for about a mile. From there it goes into Minto-Brown Island Park. The park consists of forested areas, agricultural fields and lowlands near the Willamette River. When the Willamette River used to flood, it would make "islands" here. Made up of Browns Island and Minto Island, this park is unique in that it employs commercial farming as part of the recreational enjoyment of the park and as such has a "tenant farmer". The park is made up of corn and wheat fields, lots of blackberry bushes and many stands of cottonwood trees mixed in with a few maples. This path is a great way to get away from the rush of the city with its laid back rural feel. It's especially pretty on the part that runs alongside the Willamette River. There are quite a few picnic spots and a nice playground here.

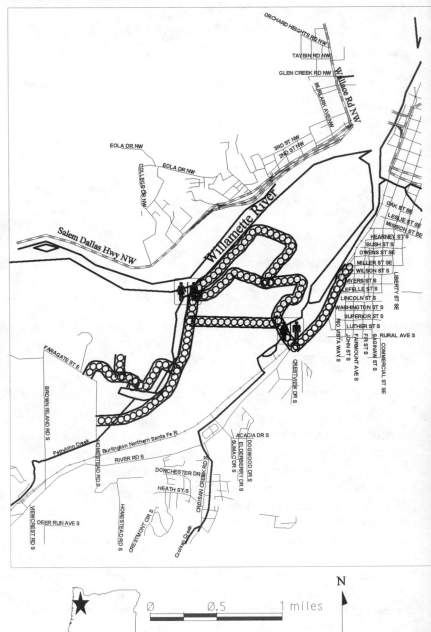

N

http://www.PedalPals.com/

Table 42-1. Path Data

Distance	City	County	Cost	Maps	Setting
3.6 mi.	Sublimity	Marion	state park entrance fee	H, U	Park

Table 42-2. Path Data

Path Surface	Internet
8 ft asphalt	*http://www.oregonstateparks.org*

Lots of shade among the tall trees

Getting There: On I-5 in Salem, head east on Highway 22 and follow the signs to Silver Falls State Park.

This path runs through the beautiful forests and meadows of this park, Oregon's biggest and possibly most diverse state park. Situated in the foothills of the Cascades, this park has it all - ten waterfalls, hiking trails, horse trails, bike paths, a campground, historic buildings and a conference center.

Starting at the campground, the path passes under Highway 214 and follows the South Fork of Silver Creek on its west bank past the swimming area on the opposite bank. It then turns right to cross the creek and goes through the parking area. Turn left when you enter the parking area and find a short path toward the lodge. Stay on the service road until it splits, straight ahead you'll see a bike path sign. It then goes through a wooded area, crosses Highway 214 and forms a loop that is beautifully wooded but has some meadow areas also. The paths around the lodge are not marked very well and it's hard to tell if a particular path is for bikers, walkers, or both. When it's crowded here, it's probably a good idea to stick to the route outlined above.

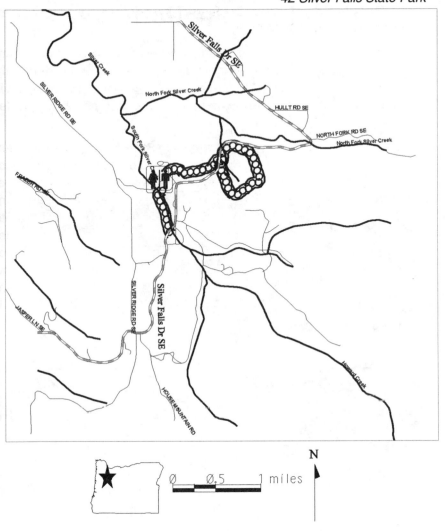

N

Ø   Ø,5   1 miles

43 Periwinkle Bike Path

Table 43-1. Path Data

Distance	City	County	Map	End1	End2	Setting
3.4 mi.	Albany	Benton	J	S. Hill St & 12th Ave.	Albany High School	City

Table 43-2. Path Data

Path Surface
8 ft asphalt, concrete on Waverly Dr.

Table 43-3. Path Data

Internet
http://www.ci.albany.or.us/pages/parks_and_rec/pr_frameset.html

Out for a scoot

Getting There: Take I-5 Exit #233, go west on Santiam Hwy for a little over one half mile then turn left (south) on Waverly Drive for one half mile to Grand Prairie Park on the right (west).

This very cute neighborhood path starts at the Boys & Girls Club. It then follows the Periwinkle Creek passing through Periwinkle Park and then to Grand Prairie Park. There, it turns into a widened sidewalk running north and south along the west side of Waverly Drive. Be careful along this widened sidewalk as there are many driveways and blind spots.

N

http://www.PedalPals.com/

44 West Corvallis

Table 44-1. Path Data

Distance	City	County	Map	End1	End2
4.3 mi.	Corvallis	Benton	I	Walnut Blvd & Witham Hill Dr.	Country Club Dr. & 53rd St.

Table 44-2. Path Data

Setting	Path Surface
City	8 ft concrete

Along 53rd south of the Benton County fairgrounds

Getting There: From downtown Corvallis, head west on Harrison Street for about two and one half miles to Walnut Blvd.

For the most part, this path is used primarily by commuters as it has many conflicts, especially in the southern half. The northwest spur winds through Walnut Park with its nice picnic area and playground.

The path starts at the Riverfront Path and heads north as a widened sidewalk passing the Midge Cramer/Campus Way Path, Benton County Fairgrounds and then ending in Walnut Park. Watch out for the many driveway crossings south of Harrison Street.

http://www.PedalPals.com/

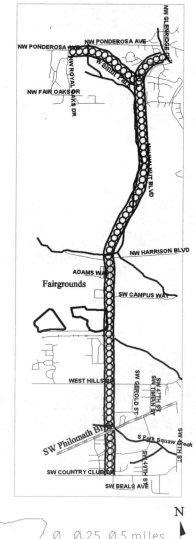

NW GLENRIDGE

NW PONDEROSA AVE

NW PONDEROSA

NW ROYAL OAKS DR

NW FAIR OAKS DR

Walnut Pari

NW WALNUT BLVD

NW HARRISON BLVD

ADAMS WA

Fairgrounds

SW CAMPUS WAY

WEST HILLS

SW GEROLD ST

SW 47TH ST

SW TIMIAN ST

SW PHILOMATH BLVD

S Fork Squaw Creek

SW 48TH ST

SW 49TH S

SW COUNTRY CLUB DR

SW BEALS AVE

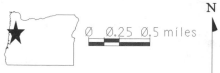

N

Ø   Ø.25 Ø.5 miles

45 Riverfront Path

Table 45-1. Path Data

Distance	Cities	County	Maps	End1	End2
7.4 mi.	Corvallis, Philomath	Benton	H, I	2nd & Tyler, Corvallis	Applegate St, Philomath

Table 45-2. Path Data

Setting	Path Surface
City, Rural	mostly 8 ft asphalt, some 10 ft concrete

The Willamette River from the Riverfront Path

Getting There: Park as close to the river in downtown Corvallis as you can get. Alternately, start in Philomath by heading west on Highway 20

http://www.PedalPals.com/

from Corvallis for six miles then turn left (south) on Newton Street and park.

This path is the pride and joy of Corvallis, representing a great deal of good planning and aesthetic value. Linking Corvallis with the neighboring community of Philomath, it's a great path for commuting and recreation.

Starting from downtown, this path skirts the west bank of the Willamette River. This section passes near many restaurants and retail shops. It then heads west along Mary's River through Avery Park. Leaving Mary's River, it goes near a research park and then runs alongside Highway 20, climbing a small hill where you will get great views of Mary's Peak directly west. Into Philomath, it turns into a greenway that runs along Newton Creek and ends at the high school. Corvallis is currently thinking about revamping the riverfront portion of this path.

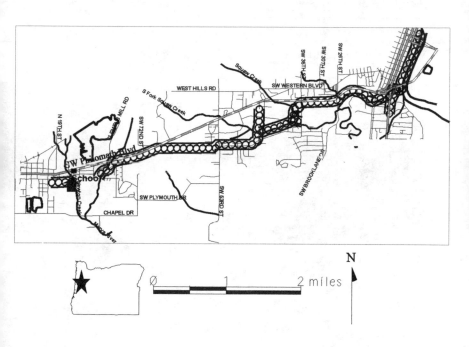

46 Campus Way/Midge Cramer

Table 46-1. Path Data

Distance	City	County	Maps	End1	End2
3.2 mi.	Corvallis	Benton	H, I	Bald Hill Park	Campus Way & 35th, Oregon State University

Table 46-2. Path Data

Setting	Path Surface
City, Rural	11-24 ft asphalt

The Irish Bend Covered Bridge on Campus Way path.

Getting There: From downtown Corvallis, head west on Harrison Street for about one and one half miles, then turn left (south) on 35th Street and go less than one half mile to Campus Way.

This is a very scenic path that meanders through OSU agricultural land and then the grasslands of Bald Hill Park. Starting at OSU heading straight west, it enters OSU Animal Sciences Livestock Facilities, a huge tract of land west of OSU mostly made up of open pasture. In the middle of this, you will pass through the historic Irish Bend Covered Bridge. The path then takes a short jog at 53rd Street and then the Midge Cramer bike path starts. This path was named in honor of Midge Cramer and his many years of volunteer service to advance bicycle transportation in the state and the region. It goes by the Benton County fairgrounds and climbs up the side of Bald Hill. From here, it branches into two segments. The north segment passes a barn shelter and Mulkey Creek near the end at Oak Creek Road. The south segment goes to Reservoir Road. Campus Way/Midge Cramer is also used by countless bikers to get to the mountain bike trails in Bald Hill Park.

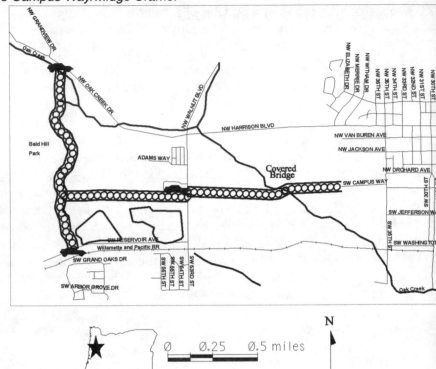

http://www.PedalPals.com/

47 Corvallis Hwy 99

Table 47-1. Path Data

Distance	City	County	Map	End1	End2
1.0 mi.	Corvallis	Benton	I	Circle Blvd & Hwy 99	Buchanan Ave. & 8th St.

Table 47-2. Path Data

Setting	Path Surface
City	12 ft concrete

Alongside Highway 99

Getting There: From downtown Corvallis, park near Buchanan Avenue and 9th Street.

This path doesn't seem to be very useful. I'm not sure who would use it, maybe a possible commute to Hewlett Packard.

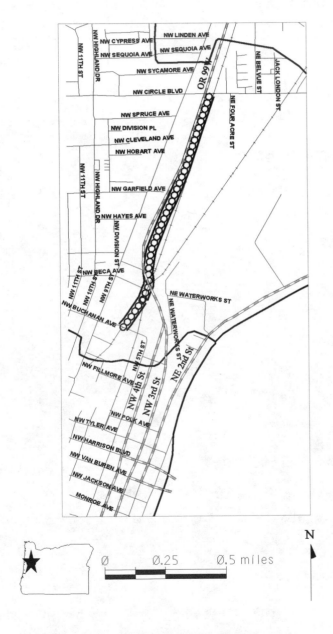

N

Part 4. South Willamette Valley

Consisting of Eugene, Springfield, and Cottage Grove, this part has a lot of variety to offer. The paths in Eugene alone run the gamut from lovely river paths to a long rural path and more bike bridges than you can imagine.

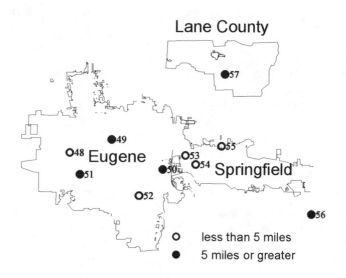

48 Roosevelt Blvd/Beltline

Table 48-1. Path Data

Distance	City	County	Map	End1	End2
4.1 mi.	Eugene	Lane	L	Royal Ave & Beltline	Roosevelt Blvd. & Maple

Table 48-2. Path Data

Setting	Path Surface
City	8 ft asphalt

Table 48-3. Path Data

Internet
http://www.ci.eugene.or.us/pw/bike/default.htm

A nice neighborhood walk

Getting There: From downtown Eugene, head north on 99W then turn right on Chambers Street. Go one half mile to Roosevelt Blvd, turn left (west) and go for about one mile. Park near Maple and Roosevelt.

This is primarily a commute path to get from some parts of west Eugene to downtown and along the west side of Eugene's Beltline Highway.

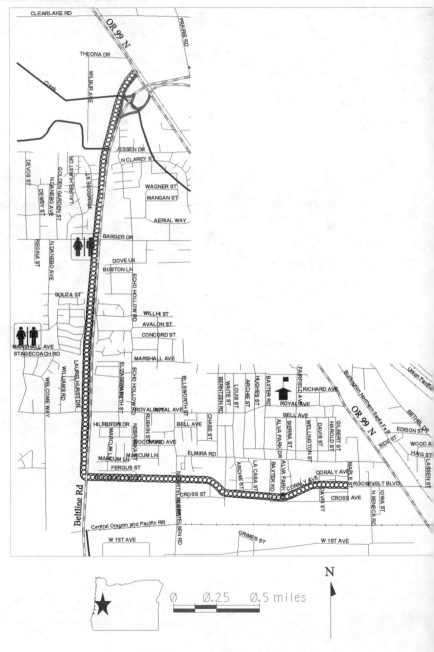

http://www.PedalPals.com/

49 Willamette River Trail-West

Table 49-1. Path Data

Distance	City	County	Map	End1	End2
8.8 mi.	Eugene	Lane	L	River Rd.	Coburg Rd & Willamette River

Table 49-2. Path Data

Setting	Path Surface
River Greenway	8-10 ft asphalt

Table 49-3. Path Data

Internet
http://www.ci.eugene.or.us/pw/bike/default.htm

On the south bank of the Willamette River

Getting There: There are numerous access points on this trail (see map), a popular one is the parking lot at the Rose Garden. To reach it, take I-105 to the end, then turn right (west) at the light and take an immediate right (north) turn at Madison. Take Madison Street north to the end. Another good spot is the Valley River Center (VRC) Mall, follow the signs on I-105.

This path, along with the Willamette River Trail-East, represents Eugene's finest, the almost perfect greenway paths that serve a very wide mix of users. These two paths are very popular and form a veritable freeway through the heart of Eugene and into Springfield. There are numerous opportunities for a picnic along these paths and lots of spots for you to explore the river bank.

Starting on the south side of the DeFazio Bike Bridge next to Ferry Street Bridge (Coburg Road), the path heads northwest, hugging the Willamette River and enters Skinner Butte Park. Here you can leave the path and, given enough energy, pedal up a steep street to the top of Skinner Butte for a excellent view of the city. Just past this park is the Owen Rose Gardens with its very wide variety of roses. From here, the path passes the Greenway Bike Bridge (to VRC) and then continues along the bank ending at the sewage treatment plant. You can also go over the Owosso Bike Bridge at the north end and head down on the northeast side of the Willamette River past Marist High School where the path continues through a protected wetland and past Valley River Center Mall. It then gets sandwiched between the river and I-105 for about three quarters of a mile. This is the only stretch on the river pathways where the noise is high.

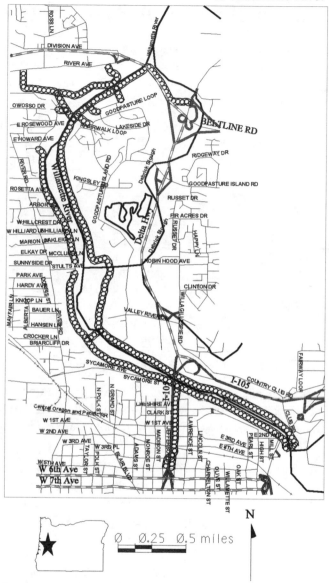

50 Willamette River Trail-East

Table 50-1. Path Data

Distance	Cities	County	Map	End1
11.4 mi.	Eugene, Springfield	Lane	L	Coburg Rd & Willamette River

Table 50-2. Path Data

End2	Setting	Path Surface
D Street, Springfield	River Greenway	8-10 ft asphalt

Table 50-3. Path Data

Internet
http://www.ci.eugene.or.us/pw/bike/default.htm

Getting There: There are many access points on this trail, the primary one being Alton Baker Park. Take the Centenial Blvd exit from I-105 and almost immediately take a right (south) turn onto Club Road, then a quick left into Alton Baker Park.

See general info on Willamette River Trail-West. This segment of the river trail starts at the huge Alton Baker Park. It then goes east and passes the Autzen Bike Bridge which you can take to the University of Oregon. Shortly after this point, the path forks and you have 3 routes to choose from to get to a point just east of I-5. One route goes right along the river which is very picturesque. The second route is an old road and goes through the middle of grassland just west of I-5. The third route heads north by a pond, turns east and hugs the Canoe Canal. The first and second routes pass the Knickerbocker Bike Bridge where you will find a memorial to Willie Knickerbocker, considered the "Father of bicycling in Eugene". The third path connects with another path that heads north along I-5 and then Garden Way. This is the best way to get to Gateway Mall from Eugene. Another way to get to Gateway Mall is along the widened sidewalk that forms part of a loop around Alton Baker Park next to Centennial Boulevard. If you continue on any of the above three paths, you will pass through a pretty wooded section and then end at D Street in Springfield.

Bridge across the Canoe Canal

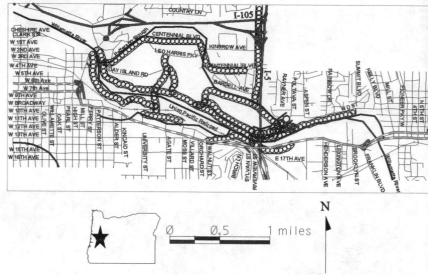

http://www.PedalPals.com/

51 Fern Ridge Trail

Table 51-1. Path Data

Distance	City	County	Map	End1	End2
5.4 mi.	Eugene	Lane	L	Terry Dr. north of 11th	15th & Jefferson St.

Table 51-2. Path Data

Setting	Path Surface
City & Rural, Creek Greenway	8 ft asphalt, 10 ft concrete

Table 51-3. Path Data

Internet
http://www.ci.eugene.or.us/pw/bike/default.htm

Getting There: From downtown Eugene, go west on 11th Avenue and then turn right (south) on Polk Street. Park around 22nd Avenue.

This path became a pet project of a local legislator and, as such, has had a lot of attention. A new fully lighted section has recently been added that extended it to its current length. Used as a commute path during the weekdays, this path is also very popular for recreational users during the weekends.

Starting near the Jefferson Middle School, the path passes by a disc golf course, then goes over 18th Street on a new bike bridge. It then turns west to head out along Amazon Creek. You'll find ducks, herons and even nutrias along the Amazon. On a clear day, check out the view of the Three Sisters Mountains from the old railroad trestle pictured above just west of Oak Patch Street. You will then pass a chocolate factory and later a wetland restoration area and finally end at Terry Street. There are several short signed walking trails through the adjacent wetlands. Plans are to extend this path out to Fern Ridge Reservoir (hence the name).

A good use for an old railroad trestle

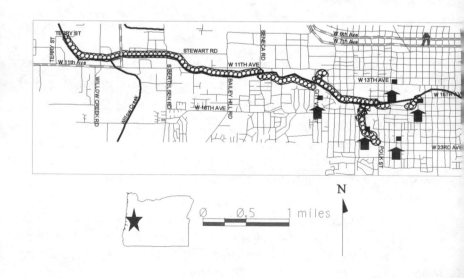

52 Amazon Trail

Table 52-1. Path Data

Distance	City	County	Map	End1	End2
1.6 mi.	Eugene	Lane	L	South Eugene High School	34th Place & Hilyard St.

Table 52-2. Path Data

Setting	Path Surface
City, Creek Greenway	10 ft concrete

Table 52-3. Path Data

Internet
http://www.ci.eugene.or.us/pw/bike/default.htm

Just south of South Eugene High School

Getting There: From downtown Eugene, go south on Hilyard and park in the Amazon Community Center's parking lot (south of 24th Street).

This very popular path gets used by lots of exercise enthusiasts all year long and Amazon Pool users during the summer. It connects the many neighborhoods south of South Eugene High School with the school itself. It runs through Amazon Park with a large play area, picnic area, and wading pool. North of Amazon Park is Amazon Pool. Amazon Pool has been newly remodeled with an Olympic size pool, water slides and multiple diving levels. South of Amazon Pool and Park is the skateboard park.

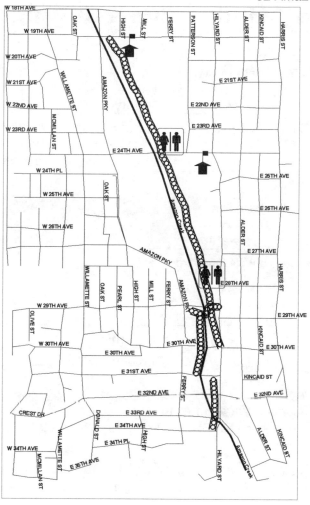

53 By-Gully Bike & Jogging Path

Table 53-1. Path Data

Distance	City	County	Map	End1	End2
1.3 mi.	Springfield	Lane	L	Anderson St. & Quinalt St.	Pioneer Parkway & I-105

Table 53-2. Path Data

Setting	Path Surface
Near busy 4 lane expressway	8 ft asphalt

Table 53-3. Path Data

Internet
http://www.ci.eugene.or.us/pw/bike/default.htm

Getting There: From Highway 126, exit on Pioneer Parkway and head south for one quarter mile. Turn right on Centennial Blvd., go two blocks and turn right on Mill Street. Then go four blocks to Fariview and park on the street.

This path is far enough from busy Highway 126 so that noise is not too much of a problem. It connects neighborhoods up with the Pioneer Parkway.

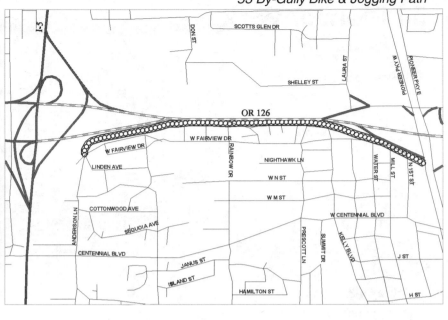

OR 126

N

Ø   Ø.25   Ø.5 miles

54 Pioneer Parkway

Table 54-1. Path Data

Distance	City	County	Map	End1	End2
1.7 mi.	Springfield	Lane	L	Harlow Rd.	B Street

Table 54-2. Path Data

Setting	Path Surface
Middle of wide boulevard	8 ft asphalt

Table 54-3. Path Data

Internet
http://www.ci.eugene.or.us/pw/bike/default.htm

Right down the middle of the boulevard.

http://www.PedalPals.com/

Getting There: From I-5, take Highway 126 east and take the first exit (Pioneer Parkway). Go north and park in the shopping area on the right.

Starting as a widened sidewalk in downtown Springfield, this path crosses many streets and then spends the rest of its time in the median of a very wide (almost a greenway) boulevard. Note that the connection from this path to the EWEB path requires you to cross north bound Pioneer at Q Street and then proceed north along a very old widened sidewalk to the EWEB path.

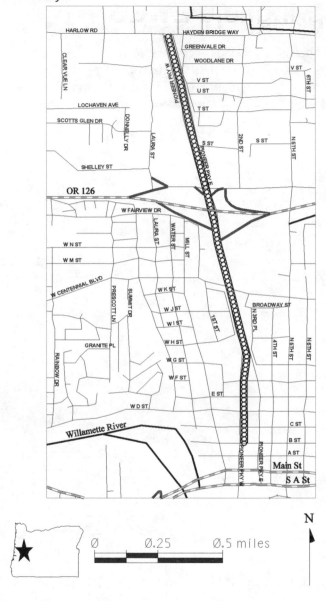

http://www.PedalPals.com/

55 Springfield EWEB

Table 55-1. Path Data

Distance	City	County	Map	End1	End2
2.6 mi.	Springfield	Lane	L	Pioneer Parkway	35th St. near Yolanda St.

Table 55-2. Path Data

Setting	Path Surface
City, easement	8 ft asphalt

Table 55-3. Path Data

Internet
http://www.ci.eugene.or.us/pw/bike/default.htm

Getting There: From I-5, take Highway 126 east and take the first exit (Pioneer Parkway). Turn left (north) and park in the shopping area on the right.

This straight as an arrow path runs along an electric company's easement that heads mostly east between back yards and then out into the open country toward Hayden Bridge.

Along the Eugene Water and Electric Board right-of-way

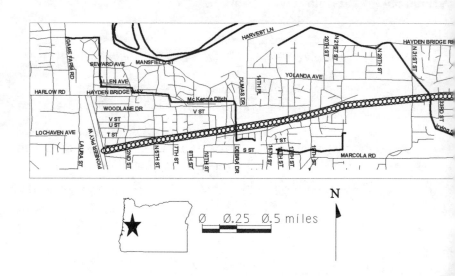

N

Ø   Ø.25   Ø.5 miles

56 Booth Kelly Logging Road

Table 56-1. Path Data

Distance	City	County	End1	End2	Setting
5.0 mi.	Springfiled	Lane	57th St.	Hills Creek Rd.	Private logging road

Table 56-2. Path Data

Path Surface
20 ft asphalt

Getting There: The real start is on the east side 57th Street about a mile south of Main Street but there is very limited parking here. A better access is from the east end of Mt. Vernon Road. Take Highway 126 east to 58th Street. Turn right on 58th Street (after a few blocks it becomes 57th Street), then go one half mile to the end and turn left on Mt. Veron Road and take it to the end and park on the street.

Strictly speaking, this is not a path but a Weyerhaeuser logging road so be aware that you may see a rare logging truck on this road. This road is not maintained so expect some tree debris on the road. This road is private and as such the rules concerning it's use could change. Please pay attention to signs that you see at the gates.

A bit steep during the first 2 miles, it then stays fairly level the rest of the way. It has some great views of the valley around Jasper. You will need to go around the gate when you get to Wallace Creek Road. After crossing Wallace Creek Road the road is open to vehicles for about one half mile. When you get just past the cemetery you will need to go around another gate. From here you can go to the last gate and turn around.

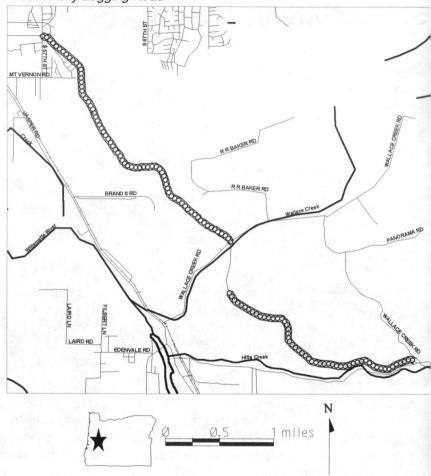

N

57 Row River

Table 57-1. Path Data

Distance	Cities	County	Maps	End1	End2	Setting
16.1 mi.	Cottage Grove, Dorena, Culp Creek	Lane	K, V	10th St. & Main St, Cottage Grove	Culp Creek	Rail to Trail

Table 57-2. Path Data

Path Surface	Internet
8-12 ft asphalt	*http://www.edo.or.blm.gov/rec/Row_trail/*

Getting There: Take I-5 Exit #174 and head west on the Cottage Grove Connector. Go for about one mile then turn left (south) on Highway 99. Go for 2 miles and park near Main Street.

Snuggled in the beautiful rolling hills of the south end of the Willamette Valley, this path features a nice mix of canopied trees, lake side bluffs, open meadows, swampy bogs, old railroad trestles and rustic covered bridges. The name Row comes from a land dispute quarrel in the 1850's but oddly enough its pronunciation rhymes with "cow". It's both one of the longest and prettiest paths in the state. One of the few rails-to-trails in the state, it started its life as the Oregon, Pacific and Eastern Railway in 1902 and was subsequently acquired by the BLM in 1994.

Beginning in Cottage Grove, the path goes by several retail shopping areas before heading out of town. After passing the Dorena Dam, the high point on the very gently sloping path, the path skirts the east side of beautiful Dorena Lake. It then goes by Harms Park, the best place for a picnic. From here, you will go past Bake Stewart Park and then Dorena. Just before the end at Culp Creek, you will come across the only chance for a drink outside of Cottage Grove, a small market on the other side of the road.

Trestle over Mosby Creek

http://www.PedalPals.com/

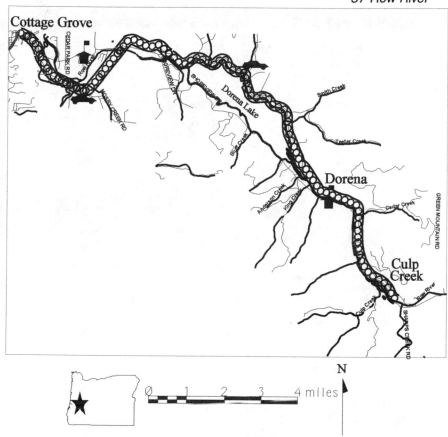

Part 5. South Oregon

This part includes Roseburg, Medford, Ashland, Klamath Falls, and Diamond Lake.

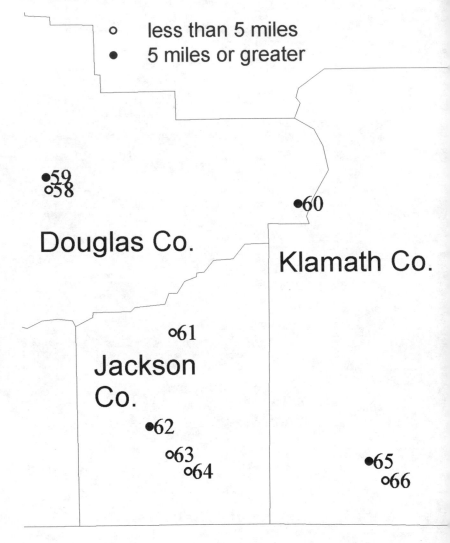

o   less than 5 miles

●   5 miles or greater

●59
o58

●60

Douglas Co.

Klamath Co.

o61

Jackson
Co.

●62

o63
o64

●65
o66

58 Roseburg I-5

Table 58-1. Path Data

Distance	City	County	Map	End1	End2
4.0 mi.	Roseburg	Douglas	M	north end of Kendall St.	Garden Valley Blvd. & I-5

Table 58-2. Path Data

Setting	Path Surface
Adjacent busy 4 lane expressway	8 ft asphalt

Table 58-3. Path Data

Internet
http://www.co.douglas.or.us/countyinfo/bike.html
http://members.rosenet.net/roseburg/parks.html

Getting There: Take I-5 Exit #125 and head east on NE Garden Valley Blvd for a few blocks and turn right (south) on Highland Street. Take it to the end.

This path is a bit noisy when you're at the same level as I-5 but not too bad when you are lower than the freeway. Starting at the end of Kendall Street, the path heads along but below the I-5 road level. When you come to Harvard Avenue, you need to cross and turn left (west) and proceed to the right of the I-5 entrance ramp where you will find the continuation of the path. From here, it continues along I-5 and passes over the Umpqua River under the I-5 bridge. This is a good example of how to integrate a path into a noisy road. The path is underneath the road level and not at the same level with all of the noise.

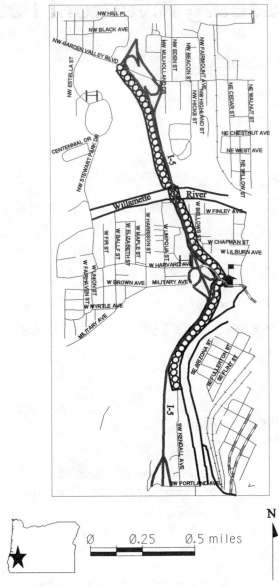

N

Ø   Ø.25   Ø.5 miles

59 Roseburg Riverfront Path

Table 59-1. Path Data

Distance	City	County	Map	End1	End2
6.0 mi.	Roseburg	Douglas	M	Near Douglas Ave. & Stephens St.	Parking lot at south end of Goetz St.

Table 59-2. Path Data

Setting	Path Surface
City	8 ft asphalt

Table 59-3. Path Data

Internet
http://www.co.douglas.or.us/countyinfo/bike.html
http://members.rosenet.net/roseburg/parks.html

Getting There: Take I-5 Exit #125 and head west on NE Garden Valley Blvd for a little under a mile. Then turn left (south) on Goetz Street. Park in the parking lot at the end of the street in Stewart Park.

This is the nicer of the two paths in Roseburg as it passes through many greenway like areas and avoids busy roads. Starting at the parking lot on Goetz Street, the path goes by Park Lake, then enters Stewart Park with its playground and shelter. Head east here and follow the north side of the river and go into River Front Park where there is a disc golf course. The path then goes through Gaddis Park and curves around with the river bend through a very nice natural area between the Umpqua River and the railroad tracks.

Steam locomotive in Stewart Park

http://www.PedalPals.com/

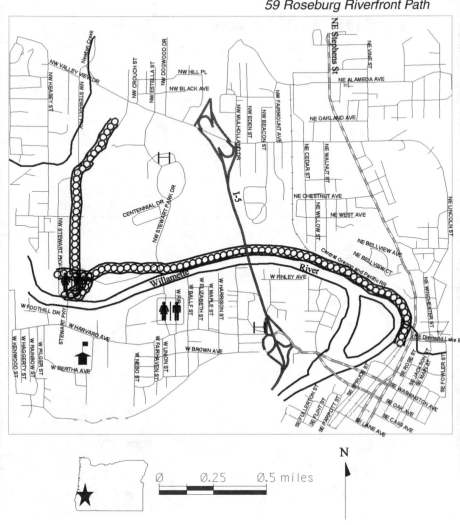

60 John Dellenback Trail

Table 60-1. Path Data

Distance	City	County	Map	Setting	Path Surface
8.9 mi.	Diamond Lake	Douglas	W	National Forest	8 ft asphalt

Table 60-2. Path Data

Internet
http://www.fs.fed.us/r6/umpqua/rec/hiking/trails/tr3_1460.html

Mt. Thielsen over Diamond Lake

Getting There: From the north, take I-5 to Eugene, then take Highway 58 to Highway 97 to Highway 138. From the south, either take Highway 97 or I-5 to Highway 62 to Highway 230 to Highway 138.

The thing that makes this path really unique is that it is set in a National Forest. Situated in the beautiful Umpqua National Forest, this somewhat hilly loop around Diamond Lake will dazzle you with great views of Mt. Thielsen, Mt. Bailey, and the lovely stands of forests that it navigates through. For most people, the car trip to Diamond Lake is a long one so it's hard to justify such a long period in the car for the bike ride. If your vacation plans call for passing by this area, by all means stop by and ride some of this path. It will be well worth it!

Starting at Diamond Lake Resort, the path snakes through the very large campground. Then it passes a memorial to John Dellenback and goes through a wetland at the south end of the lake. As it enters the west side of the lake, it climbs a bit and gets farther away from the lake as it skirts around some summer homes. Just before rounding the northwest corner, the path crosses the road and gets very close to the lake for some really nice views. As it continues around the north side of the lake, it gets a little hilly but is snug with the shore until it reaches Diamond Lake Resort. If you are only doing part of this path, go counter clockwise from the resort as the part through the campgrounds is not very special.

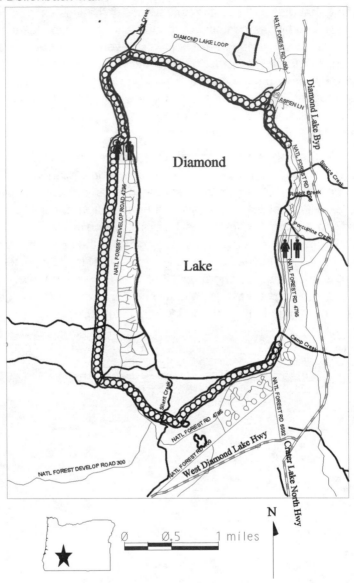

http://www.PedalPals.com/

61 Joseph Stewart State Park

Table 61-1. Path Data

Distance	City	County	Cost	Map	Setting
3.5 mi.	Trail	Jackson	state park entrance fee	U	Park

Table 61-2. Path Data

Path Surface	Internet
8 ft asphalt	*http://www.oregonstateparks.org*

Lost Creek Reservoir

Getting There: From the north, take I-5 to Exit #45 then take Highway 234 to Highway 62. From the south, take I-5 to Exit #30 then Highway 62. Follow the signs to Joseph Stewert State Park.

61 Joseph Stewart State Park

This park in the Upper Rogue Valley is home to bald eagle, osprey and turkey vultures. It sits on the east side of of Lost Creek Reservoir on gently slopping terrain so the views across the reservoir are very nice.

Starting at Picnic Area A, the path follows the road, crosses Lost Creek and climbs a small hill. On the way down, it crosses the boat launch entrance road. Be careful not to go too fast here as the cross traffic doesn't stop. From here it climbs a hill, crosses Floras Creek and heads up through the campground. It then forms a loop at the north end of the park through a very nicely forested area.

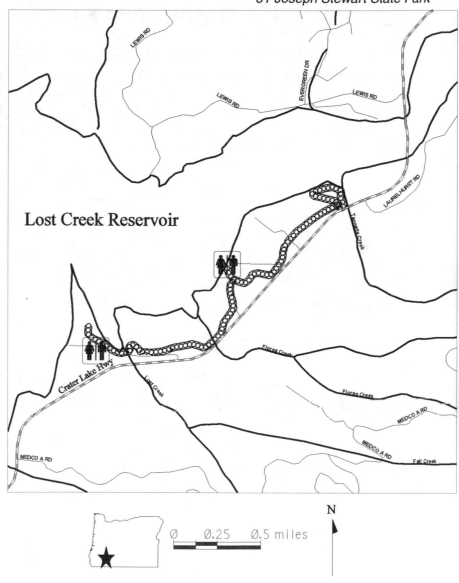

62 Bear Creek Greenway #1

Table 62-1. Path Data

Distance	City	County	Maps	End1	End2
7.6 mi.	Medford	Jackson	R, S	Pine Street near I-5, Central Point	Bear Creek Park, Medford

Table 62-2. Path Data

Setting	Path Surface
Creek Greenway	8-12 ft asphalt

Table 62-3. Path Data

Internet
http://www.mind.net/dlmark/greenway/intro.htm

Train parts at Railroad Park

Getting There: For the north end of the path (End 1), take I-5 to Exit #33 and head east on East Pine Street for about one half mile. If you want the south end of the path (End 2), take I-5 Exit #27 and go east on Barnett Road for about a half mile, then take a left (north) on Highland Drive and park in Bear Creek Park. Railroad Park is also another good place to get on this path. Take I-5 to Exit #30. Head into town (toward the Rogue Valley Mall) on Hwy 62 (Crater Lake Hwy). Get in the right hand lane and bear right onto North Pacific Hwy (Hwy 99) then, still in the right lane, onto Table Rock Road. Continue three tenths of a mile on Table Rock to the first light (Berrydale). Turn right on Berrydale, stay to the left of the entrance to Fire Station 4 and you will enter the Railroad Park parking lot.

This part of Bear Creek Greenway spends a lot of its time under or very near I-5, but overall the noise level is not too bad. It passes through lovely riparian areas next to Bear Creek and swampy bogs. When you are passing through downtown Medford on this path, you might feel like you're in Los Angeles due to the multiple layers of concrete overpasses that loom above the path, concrete-jungle style.

Starting at Bear Creek Park, the path winds through the park and then passes through downtown. From here, it is between I-5 and the creek until it comes to Highway 62 where there is branch going west to Railroad Park and a branch going near the airport, which has good views of Mt. Ashland and the Siskoyous. The path continues following I-5 to Central Point.

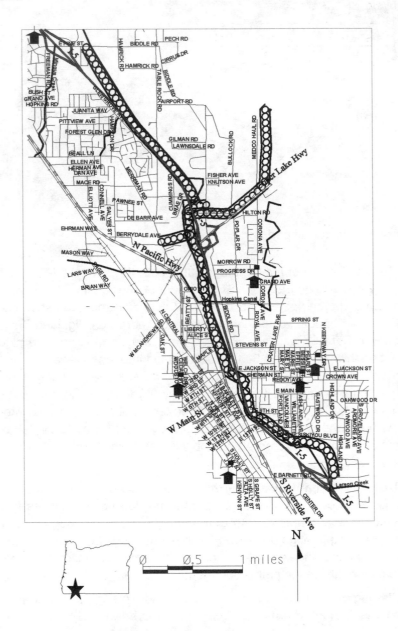

63 Bear Creek Greenway #2

Table 63-1. Path Data

Distance	Cities	County	Maps	End1	End2
4.7 mi.	Talent, Ashland	Jackson	R, S	west of West Valley View Rd & I-5	Helman St. & Nevada St, Ashland

Table 63-2. Path Data

Setting	Path Surface
Creek Greenway	10 ft asphalt

Table 63-3. Path Data

Internet
http://www.mind.net/dlmark/greenway/intro.htm

Getting There: Take I-5 to Exit #21 and go west on West Valley View Road. Park in the Valley View Mall parking lot. For the south end (End 2) of the path, take I-5 to Exit #19 and go south on South Valley View Road then immediately take a left (east) on Eagle Well Road and go for a little over two miles. Then turn right (west) on Nevada Street, take Nevada Street a few blocks to Helman Street.

Snaking through some very nice creekside areas, this part of the greenway manages to stay pretty far from I-5 but does get close to the very busy Highway 99 for a bit. Be sure to stop and write your impressions of this trail at the Bike Path Journal mailbox (see photo).

Mailbox for the Bike Path Journal

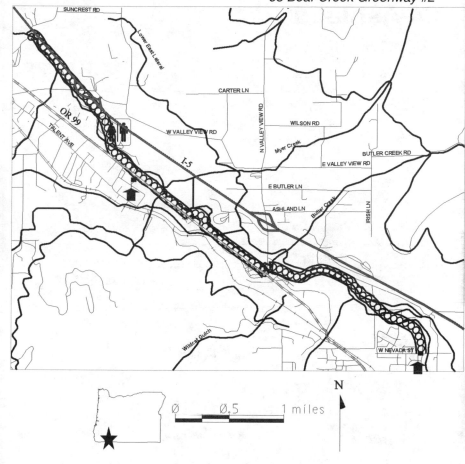

N

64 Ashland

Table 64-1. Path Data

Distance	Cities	County	Map	End1	End2
1.9 mi.	Talent, Ashland	Jackson	R	Toleman Creek Rd & Misletoe Rd	8th & "A" St.

Table 64-2. Path Data

Setting	Path Surface
City	12 ft asphalt

This path puts a smile on your face

Getting There: Take I-5 to Exit #14 and head into town (west) on Hwy 66. Turn right (south) at Tolman Creek Road, then left on Misletoe Road. Park immediately.

A nice neighborhood connector that connects parks, schools, and homes that runs alongside a railroad track. This path is in the Ashland map in the local phone book.

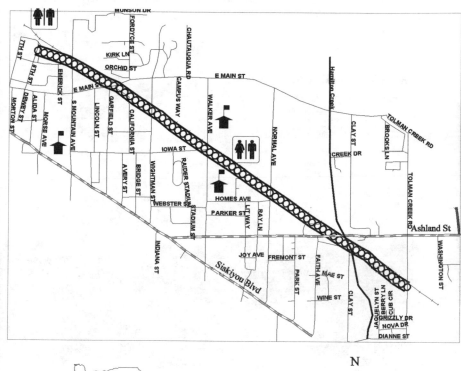

65 Klamath A Canal / Kit Carson

Table 65-1. Path Data

Distance	City	County	Map	End1	End2
5.6 mi.	Klamath Falls	Klamath	T	Espanade & Michigan	Homedale south of Harland Dr.

Table 65-2. Path Data

Setting	Path Surface
Adjacent Canal	8 ft asphalt

The A Canal

Getting There: There is parking at the Oregon Institute of Technology near the intersection of Highways 97 and 39. Turn from Highway 39 and go north on Campus and look for a place to park (End 1). To get to the other end (End 2), turn south from Highway 39 onto Homedale, go for about 1 mile then find a parking place just past the canal.

This is a great commute path because it goes almost the entire length of Klamath Falls along a pleasant canal unencumbered by noise. A large percentage of Klamath Falls lives within 3/4 mile of this path and it connects many schools and the Oregon Institute of Technology.

Starting at Homedale, the path is on a slightly raised dike that makes up the "A" Canal. It follows the canal all the way to Espanade where it turns to a widened sidewalk and crosses the canal, then heads up alongside Highway 39 for a short distance. It then parallels the street until it reaches the Oregon Institute of Technology.

http://www.PedalPals.com/

Table 66-1. Path Data

Distance	City	County	Maps	End1	End2
3.3 mi.	Klamath Falls	Klamath	T, U	Washburn Way just south of Highway 39	Highway 39 just south of Hagar Way

Table 66-2. Path Data

Setting	Path Surface	Internet
Rail to Trail	8 ft asphalt	*http://www.oregonstateparks.org* *http://www.u-r-here.com/OCE/*

Getting There: From Business 39, go south on Washburn Way. Go for one half mile and turn left on Crosby, then go to the parking lot on the left (north).

This rails-to-trails path offers a lot of potential as it is the longest linear park in Oregon at 100 miles. Currently only 3.3 miles are paved although there are plans to pave an additional 3.8 miles to bring the east end of the paved path to Olene.

From Washburn Way, the path heads straight southeast crossing the "A" Canal and then over the 1898 steel railroad bridge. Then it continues on into the country to end at Highway 39.

Oregon, California, and Eastern Railway caboose

N

Ø   Ø.5   1 miles

Part 6. East Oregon

The paths in this section are scattered far and wide in Eastern Oregon

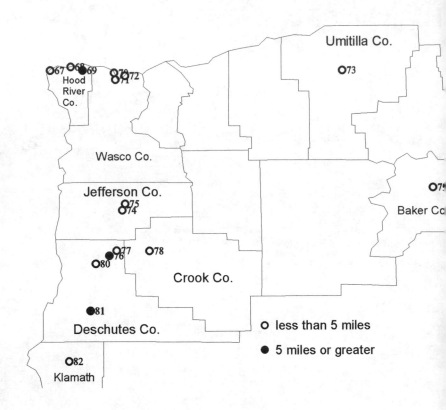

67 The Historic Columbia River Highway State Trail #1

Table 67-1. Path Data

Distance	City	Counties	Cost	Maps
3.0 mi.	Cascade Locks	Hood River, Multnomah	state park entrance fee	U, X

Table 67-2. Path Data

Setting	Path Surface	Internet
Partly adjacent busy 4 lane expressway	12 ft asphalt	*http://www.odot.state.or.us/hcrh*

Getting There: Take either I-84 Exits #40, #41, or #44 (see map). From Exit #40, turn right (south) and follow the signs to the parking lot, this may require a fee. From Exit #41, park near the fish hatchery. From Exit #44, head toward Cascade Locks for about one half mile and on the left, right alongside the I-84 west bound entrance ramp will be a parking lot that may requre a fee. This is where the path begins. There is another parking area at this exit at the Cascade Locks Trailhead parking lot under the Bridge of the Gods in Cascade Locks. No fee is required here yet.

This fairly hilly path has some awesome views of the Columbia River and of the Bonneville Dam but its beauty is tempered somewhat by its close proximity to the rumble of I-84. Starting in Cascade Locks, this path goes under I-84 then crosses Ruckle Creek on a very old bridge, goes by the fish hatchery, crosses Eagle Creek, then lastly the Bonneville Dam comes into full view. About midpoint on the path is a three flight stairway that has wheel guides so that you can place your bicycle wheels and push your bike up the staircase. Obviously, this will not work so well for wheelchairs, large tricycles, or two wheel bike trailers.

Beacon Rock as seen from across the Columbia River

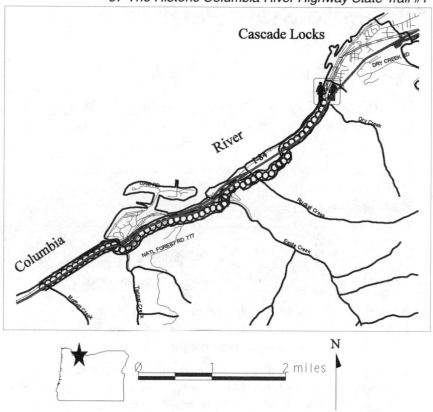

N

68 Viento State Park

Table 68-1. Path Data

Distance	City	County	Cost	Map	Setting
1.0 mi.	Wyeth	Hood River	state park entrance fee	U	Park

Table 68-2. Path Data

Path Surface	Internet
8 ft asphalt	*http://www.oregonstateparks.org*

Getting There: Take I-84 Exit #56 and follow the signs to Viento State Park. Park in the parking lot and ride or walk under I-84. Look for the start of the path on the right, just past the exit ramp.

Starting out as a gravel path, it quickly turns to asphalt, running on a beautifully canopied section of the old highway. The path ends at Starvation Creek State Park where 148 holiday railroad passengers and crew were stranded for 3 weeks during a big snow storm in 1884. The name is somewhat of an exaggeration since no one actually starved.

Starvation Creek Falls

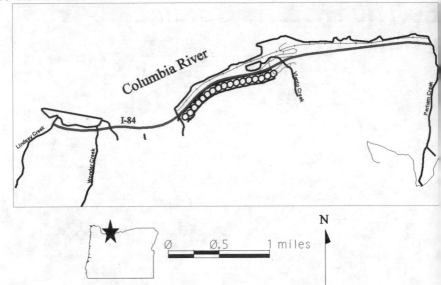

http://www.PedalPals.com/

Table 69-1. Path Data

Distance	City	Counties	Maps	Setting	Path Surface
5.0 mi.	Hood River	Hood River, Sherman	U, X	Rural Park	12 ft asphalt

Table 69-2. Path Data

Internet
http://www.odot.state.or.us/hcrh

The signature wooden fence of the Columbia River Highway

Getting There: Take I-84 Exit #64 (Highway 35) and head south on Highway 35. Turn right on the Columbia River Highway and follow this to the

Mark O. Hatfield Trailhead West.

Arguably the most scenic path in Oregon, this path's breathtaking vistas, basalt bluffs and signature wooden guardrails will tempt you into thinking it was worth every penny spent on it. It sits about 500 feet above I-84 so there is virtually no noise. On a warm summer day, this place is perfect for a picnic. It's hard to believe that this immediate area was once home to several gravel quarries.

On the west end of this path is the brand new Mark Hatfield Trailhead Visitor Center where you will find many interesting displays on the Historic Columbia River Highway and the path construction. Starting from the Visitor Center, the path goes slightly uphill through an area filled with Douglas fir, hemlock and bigleaf maple and then passes some large basalt bluffs. Later it goes through the refurbished Mosier Twin Tunnels, one of the engineering feats of the old highway.

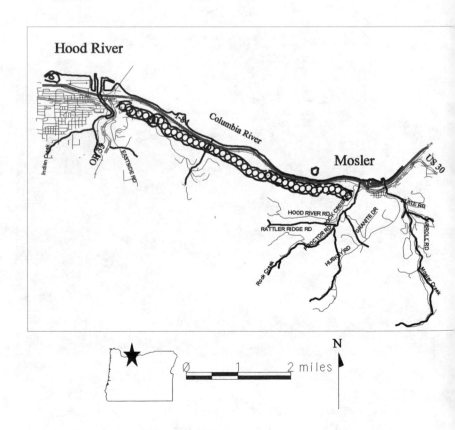

70 The Dalles Riverfront Trail #1

Table 70-1. Path Data

Distance	City	County	End1	End2	Setting
1.3 mi.	The Dalles	Wasco	Columbia Gorge Discover Center	Taylor Lake	City

Table 70-2. Path Data

Path Surface	Internet
8 ft asphalt	*http://www.thedalleschamber.com/recreation.htm*

Old wagon at the Columbia Gorge Discovery Center

Getting There: Take I-84 Exit #82 and follow the signs to the Columbia Gorge Discovery Center and park there.

The three paths in the Dalles will some day connect and make up "The Dalles Riverfront Trail". This trail will run from Columbia Gorge Discovery Center to The Dalles Dam and will be over 10 miles long. It will add a great recreation and commute resource to The Dalles.

This portion of the trail starts at the Columbia Gorge Discovery Center, passes under a railroad and runs along the Columbia River. It ends at the Taylor Lakes area. The Discovery Center is well worth a visit.

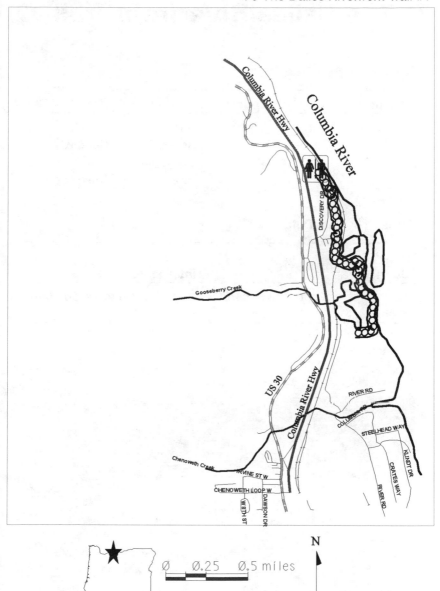

N

Ø   Ø.25   Ø.5 miles

71 The Dalles Riverfront Trail #2

Table 71-1. Path Data

Distance	City	County	End1	End2	Setting
1.0 mi.	The Dalles	Wasco	Chenowith Creek & Columbia River	River Road & Klindt Drive	City

Table 71-2. Path Data

Path Surface	Internet
10 ft asphalt	*http://www.thedalleschamber.com/recreation.htm*

The Columbia River and The Dalles in the background

Getting There: Take I-84 Exit #83 and head on 6th Street (Highway 30) toward The Dalles. Go about one block and turn left (north) on Webber Street. Take Webber Street until you get close to the river then veer left on River Road. Then take River Road to Klindt Drive, turn right on Klindt Drive and look for a parking area to your right.

See Dalles Riverfront Trail #1 for general information. This short path has nice views of the river as it heads along the Columbia River to Chenoweth Creek.

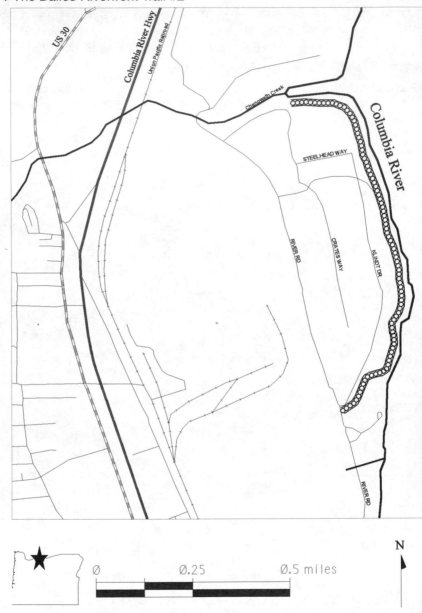

N

http://www.PedalPals.com/

Table 72-1. Path Data

Distance	City	County	End1	End2	Setting
1.2 mi.	The Dalles	Wasco	Near Seufert Park	The Dalles Dam & Visitors Center	City

Table 72-2. Path Data

Path Surface	Internet
10 ft asphalt	*http://www.thedalleschamber.com/recreation.htm*

Getting There: Take I-84 Exit #87 (Highway 197) and head north. Go a very short distance and turn right (east) on Bret Clodfelter Way and take it to the end at Seufert Park.

See Dalles Riverfront Trail #1 for general information. This short path gives nice views of The Dalles Dam with barely any I-84 noise. The railroad that runs near here used to take cargo from the sternwheelers upstream and transfer it 10 miles downstream to another sternwheeler for the trip down to Portland. Nowadays, you can ride a short piece of this trip on the tourist train "Les Dalles Portage Railroad". Check at the visitors center near The Dalles Dam.

The tourist train "Les Dalles Portage Railroad "

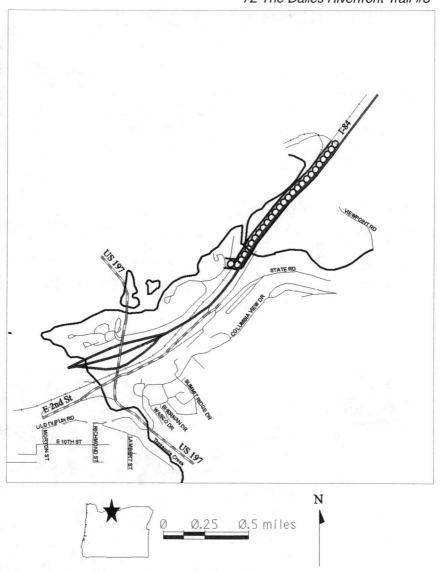

N

Ø   Ø.25   Ø.5 miles

73 Umatilla River Parkway

Table 73-1. Path Data

Distance	City	County	End1	End2	Setting
2.5 mi.	Pendleton	Umatilla	Bobwhite Field	Little league field	City

Table 73-2. Path Data

Path Surface	Internet
8 ft asphalt	*http://www.pendleton-oregon.org/entert.html*

Walking on a levee

Getting There: From the west, take I-84 Exit #207 and follow Highway

30 east for 2 miles. Park near where Highway 30 crosses the river at the boat ramp. From the east, take I-84 Exit #213 and follow Highway 30 west for about 2 miles and park near Main Street.

What started out as a levee built by the city because of recurrent flooding has become the basis for this path. It really adds a lot to this small town and is a great example for how smaller communities can reduce their automotive dependence and improve their livability. Starting from the west end of the path near the Blue Mountain Community College (End 1), the path runs along the south bank of the Umatilla River. It runs by the Convention Center and Roundup Grounds, passes through the center of town and heads out to the eastern section to end at the Little League Ballpark.

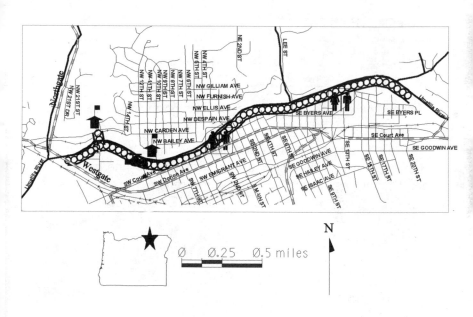

N

74 Madras Willow Creek

Table 74-1. Path Data

Distance	City	County	End1	End2	Setting
1.0 mi.	Madras	Jefferson	NE 7th St. & NE A St.	NE Kinkade Rd. & SE Grizzly Rd.	Rural Park

Table 74-2. Path Data

Path Surface
8 ft asphalt

Getting There: Madras is located 42 miles north of Bend. From Portland, take Highway 26 southeast 118 miles.

This lovely path has just recently been planted with many new trees. Running along pretty Willow Creek, it starts near the high school and heads northwest ending just north of the center of town.

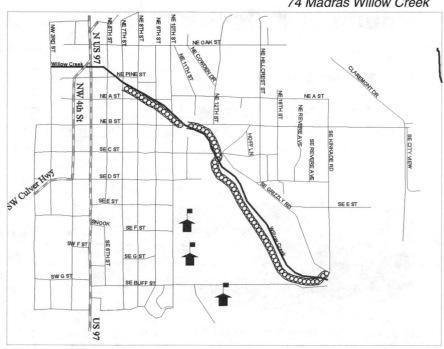

N

75 Juniper Hills Park

Table 75-1. Path Data

Distance	City	County	Setting	Path Surface
1.6 mi.	Madras	Jefferson	City	8 ft asphalt

Memorial Wall of Fossils

Getting There: Madras is located 42 miles north of Bend. From Portland, take Highway 26 southeast 118 miles. Turn left (east) at "B" Street and go a little more than a mile. Bean Park is on the left. There is as small parking lot in Bean Park.

This little loop has great views of the Three Sisters, Mt. Jefferson, and Mt. Hood on a clear day. Check out the interesting "Wall of Fossils" display along the path.

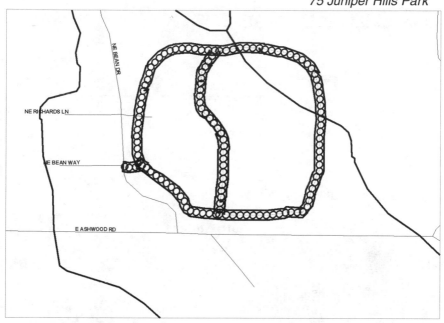

NE BEAN DR

NE RICHARDS LN

NE BEAN WAY

E ASHWOOD RD

Ø   Ø.125   Ø.25 miles

N

76 Eagle Crest

Table 76-1. Path Data

Distance	City	County	Cost	Map	Setting
6.9 mi.	Redmond	Deschutes	$3/hr $18/day	Y	Private Resort

Table 76-2. Path Data

Path Surface
8 ft asphalt

Through a golf course in the high desert

Getting There: Eagle Crest is located four miles west of Redmond. Take Highway 126 west of Redmond to Cline Falls Highway, take this south about 1 mile to the entrance.

Eagle Crest is a private resort. See Sunriver for general information about private resorts. It's easy to label Eagle Crest as a "small Sunriver" but there are some differences. Eagle Crest is less like a city, it doesn't have the grocery stores, tourist shops and toy stores that you find at Sunriver. The only difference in the bike paths is that they often turn into bike lanes (see glossary) and back into paths. It's worth noting that the paths west of Cline Falls Highway can be fairly steep so be cautioned if you have one of the one-speed bikes that are rented. The path rules here are much the same as Sunriver except that skates and skateboards are allowed.

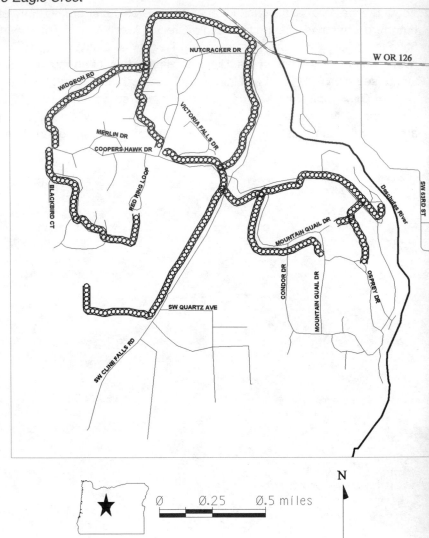

N

Ø   Ø.25   Ø.5 miles

http://www.PedalPals.com/

77 Dry Canyon

Table 77-1. Path Data

Distance	City	County	Map	End1	End2
2.0 mi.	Redmond	Deschutes	N	Fir Avenue and Canyon Drive	Sewage Treatment Plant, N.W. Pershall Way

Table 77-2. Path Data

Setting	Path Surface
Park	10 ft asphalt

Table 77-3. Path Data

Internet
http://www.insiders.com/bend/main-parks3.htm

Overview of Dry Canyon

Getting There: Redmond is 16 miles north of Bend on Highway 97. From Portland, take Highway 26 for 118 miles to Madras then go south on Highway 97 for 26 miles to Redmond. In Redmond, turn west on Fir Avenue and go the end of the street and park nearby. On the north end of the path (End 2), you can park near the sewage treatment plant. From Highway 97, go west on NW Pershall Way and turn left (south) near the treatment plant and look for the trailhead parking lot.

Made of rim rock basalt, this tiny parched canyon is home to a few struggling plants like sagebrush, Idaho fescue, and biscuitroot. The path starts near Fir Avenue and heads along the canyon floor to the treatment plant.

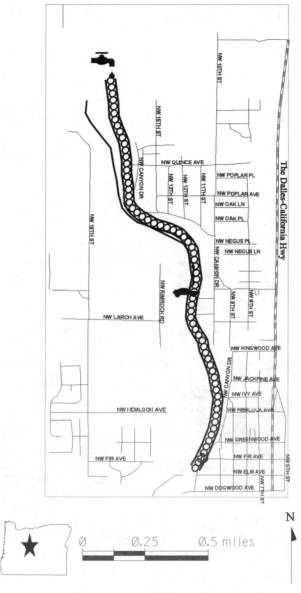

N

78 Prineville

Table 78-1. Path Data

Distance	City	County	End1	End2	Setting
1.5 mi.	Prineville	Crook	Knowledge St. & 3rd St.	Madras Hwy & 6th St.	City

Table 78-2. Path Data

Path Surface
8 ft asphalt

A late afternoon walk along the Ochoco Creek

Getting There: Prineville is located 35 miles northeast of Bend. From Portland, take Highway 29 for 146 miles to Prineville.

This path goes from one end of town to the other along the Ochoco Creek, hopping from one side of the creek to the other with some very nice parks in between. On the east end of the path (End 1), there is a great park for kids as it has a very nice play structure. Just west of Juniper Street is a skateboard park.

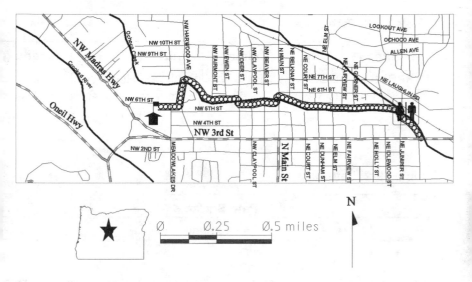

79 Leo Adler Memorial Pathway

Table 79-1. Path Data

Distance	City	County	End1	End2	Setting
1.6 mi.	Baker City	Baker	Public Library	Hughes Ln. & Kirkway St.	City

Table 79-2. Path Data

Path Surface
9 ft asphalt

The Powder River (photo by Gary Van Patten)

Getting There: Baker City is located on I-84 304 miles east of Portland and 72 miles west of Ontario. Take I-84 Exit #304 and go west on Campbell Street for one mile. Park just before Main Street.

This little greenway will enhance the once-neglected Powder River and provide both some commute and recreational opportunities for Baker City. This path was named after multimillionaire Leo Adler who built a seven-state magazine business. Part of the money he left to the city upon his death went into building this path. The path goes from the library and heads along the Powder River. It then splits, going to either Hughes Street or the Baker Sports Complex.

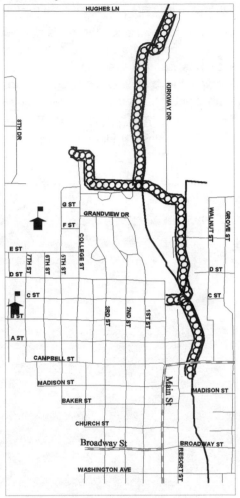

N

http://www.PedalPals.com/

80 Bend

Table 80-1. Path Data

Distance	City	County	Map	End1	End2
1.4 mi.	Bend	Deschutes	N	NW Riverside Blvd. & Carlon Ave.	Bachlor Dr. & Century Dr.

Table 80-2. Path Data

Setting	Path Surface
City	8 ft asphalt

The beautiful Deschutes River

Getting There: From Portland, take Highway 26 for 118 miles to Madras.

Then go south on Highway 97 for 42 miles to Bend.

The town known for mountain biking doesn't have too much in the way of paved paths. There's just one here. It's a little beat up and in need of repair but the spectacular Deschutes River overlook and lovely McKay Park with its rapids make it worthwhile.

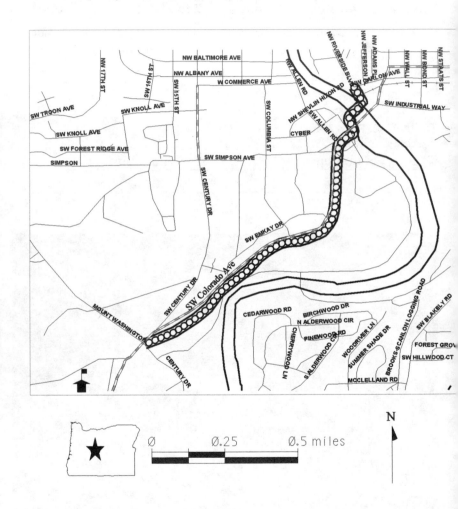

http://www.PedalPals.com/

81 Sunriver Resort

Table 81-1. Path Data

Distance	City	County	Cost	Map	Setting
37.0 mi.	Sunriver	Deschutes	$3/hour $12/day	O	Private Resort

Table 81-2. Path Data

Path Surface	Internet
8-10 ft asphalt	*http://www.sunrivernet.com/main.html*

Part of Sunriver's extensive network of paths

Getting There: Sunriver is about 13 miles south of Bend on Highway 97. There are two entrances to Sunriver, the one closest to Bend is not labeled as "Sunriver" but just "Cottonwood Road". The next entrance is the main entrance and is the one to use if you want bike rental.

Sunriver is a private resort which means that the bike paths and the streets are privately owned by the Sunriver Owners Association. While there isn't an official written policy on the bike paths, you must either be a guest or rent a bike from one of the bike rentals. It's not apparent how this rule is enforced. Being a guest means owning or renting one of the properties at Sunriver. If you want to use your own bike but aren't a guest, you could probably negotiate something with one of the bike rental places (rent a helmet?). Note that only bikes and pedestrians are allowed on the paths. Skates, skateboards, and inline skates are not allowed. Wheelchairs are okay. The paths are actually snow plowed in the winter so don't forget gloves!

Sunriver might be termed a "quasi-city" since it resembles any other town except that it's privately owned. What really makes it unique, at least from the path point of view, is that the bike paths were designed into the community initially rather than added on later in a hodgepodge fashion as is the case in most communities. This means you will be able to get just about anywhere you want on a path in the 3300 acres that make up Sunriver. It also means that there aren't a lot of conflicts with motorized vehicles.

It's unlikely that you will do the entire 30 plus miles of paths but if you're looking for a nice long ride, do all the outer perimeter paths which come to about 12.5 miles. On this ride, you will see both the residential areas and the portions of the path that go adjacent to the pretty Deschutes River which are very scenic. The map for Sunriver is too large to be included here so pick up one at any realty office or at the information office near the gas station at the main entrance to Sunriver. There are two maps. They are both good but I could read the glossy one better.

82 Crescent

Table 82-1. Path Data

Distance	Cities	County	Map	Setting	Path Surface
2.6 mi.	Crescent, Gilcrest	Klamath	N	Rural	8 ft asphalt

Highway 97 is to the right

Getting There: From Bend, take Highway 297 south for 47 miles to Crescent.

This beat up path has many wide cracks and is in need of some maintenance. Starting at Mountain View Drive, the path runs along Highway 97. Crescent Lake soon comes in view across the highway. Then the path turns into a widened sidewalk before ending at the Deschutes Ranger Station. The path also heads west at County Road 61 (also called Crescent Cutoff). This part of the path is alongside a fairly quiet county road.

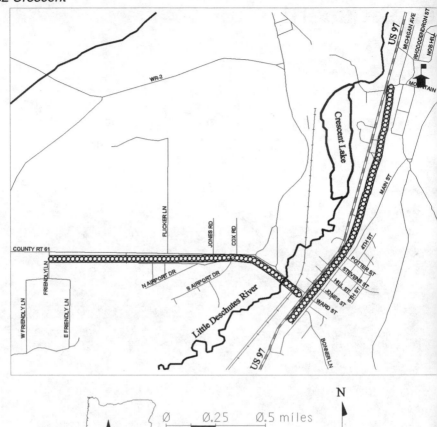

http://www.PedalPals.com/

Glossary

Bicycle Boulevard

A shared roadway. Bikes and motor vehicles share the space without marked bicycle lanes but the through movement of bicycles is given priority. This is accomplished by using traffic-calming devices (speed bumps, traffic circles, etc) to control traffic speeds and discourage through trips by motor vehicles. This book does not cover these.

Bike Lane

A lane for bicycles that is part of the road, almost always marked with a paint stripe that separates the bike portion from the auto portion. An extended shoulder that is marked with a paint stripe. This book does not cover these.

Bike Path

An off-road path used primarily by bicyclists. May or may not be paved.

Bikeway

A term used when speaking of both bike paths and bike lanes.

Conflicts

The points on a path that cross vechicular traffic including driveways, streets, alleys, etc.

Curb Cutout

Where the curb has been "flattened" to allow a ramp from the street level to the sidewalk level. Mostly used for wheelchair usage on sidewalks but also used where bike paths cross a street.

Greenway

A linear park that is usually adjacent to a river, creek, stream, or canal.

Multi Use Path

For the purpose of this book, an off-street paved path at least 8 feet wide.

Pedway

Any path that accomodates pedestrians.

Rails to Trails

An abandoned railroad track that has been converted to a multi-use path, sometimes paved or partially paved. See resources.

Transportation Equity Act

The source of funding for most multi-use paths. See Resources.

Appendix A. Maps, Resources

Where to get bike maps and information [1]

A. Bike There! (The best Portland area bike map)
   Metro Transportation Department
   600 NE Grande Ave
   Portland, OR 97232
   (503) 797-1742
   Metro: Transportation planning:
   Bike map Price: $7.00 (via internet) (http://www.metro-region.org/transpo/
   bikemap/bike.html)

B. Portland Area Bikeways
   City of Portland Office of Transportation
   1120 SW Fifth Ave., #800
   Portland, OR 97204
   (503)823-2925

C. Springwater Corridor Map
   Portland Parks & Recreation
   1120 SW Fifth Ave., #1302
   Portland, OR 97204
   (503)823-PLAY or(503)823-2223
      Portland Parks and Recreation
   - Portland, Oregon (http://www.portlandparks.org/)

D. Washington County, "Getting There by Bike"
   Washington County Visitors Association
   5075 SW Griffith Drive Suite 120
   Beaverton, OR 97005
   (503) 644-5555 or
   800-537-3149
   Price: $2.00

E. Multnomah County, "Multnomah County Bicycling Guide""
   Department of Environmental Services

1600 SE 190th Ave
Portland, OR 97233-5910
(503) 988-5050 ext. 29637
Price: Free

F. Clackamas County, "Clackamas County Bike Map"
Clackamas County Department of Transportation
9101 SE Sunnybrook Blvd
Clackamas, OR 97015
(503) 353-4400
Price: $3.50 or $5.00 to mail

G. Cycle Clark County
1300 Esther Street
Vancouver, WA 98666-9810
(360) 397-2391

H. Salem, Keizer, Marion Co., & Polk Co., "Mid-Valley Regional Bike Map"
City of Salem Public Works
555 Liberty St SE
Salem, OR 97301
(503) 588-6211
Price: $4.00

I. Corvallis & Benton County, "Corvallis Area Bikeways"
Public Works Department
PO Box 1083
Corvallis, OR 97339
(541) 757-6916
Price: Free

J. Albany & Linn County, "Albany & Mid-Willamette Valley Bicycle Map"
Albany Parks and Recreation Department
333 Broadalbin St. SW
Albany, OR 97321
(541) 917-7777
Price: $4.00

K. Lane County, "Lane County Bicycle Map"
   Lane County Public Works
   3040 North Delta Highway
   Eugene, OR 97408-1696
   (541) 682-6900
   Price: 3.00

L. Eugene & Springfield, "Eugene/Springfield Bikeways Map"
   City of Eugene Public Works
   858 Pearl St
   Eugene, OR 97401
   (541) 682-5218
   Eugene Bicycling Map (http://www.ci.eugene.or.us/pw/bike/bikesite/
   Eugenemaplink.htm)
   Price: Free

M. Roseburg & Douglas County
   "Douglas County and Roseburg Bicycle Map"
   Visitors' Information and Convention Bureau
   410 SE Spruce Street
   Roseburg, OR 97470
   (541) 672-9731
   Price: Free

N. Deschutes County, "Deschutes County Bicycling Guide"
   Deschutes County Public Works
   61150 SE 27th
   Bend, OR 97702
   (541) 388-6581
   Price: Free

O. Sunriver
   Sun River Chamber of Commerce
   P.O. Box 3246
   Sunriver, OR 97707
   (541) 593-8149

P. La Grande / Union County, Bike Route Packet

Visitors and Convention Bureau
1912 Fourth Street Suite 200
La Grande, OR 97850
(800) 848-9969
Price: Free

Q. Lincoln County, "Lincoln County Bicycle Guide"
Lincoln County Road Department
880 NE 7th Street
Newport, OR 97365
(541) 265-5747
Price: Free with self addressed stamped envelope

R. Jackson County, "Jackson County Bicycling Guide"
Jackson County Roads and Parks
200 Antelope Rd.
White City, OR 97503
(541) 774-8184
Price: $1.00

S. Welcome to Your Greenway"
Bear Creek Greenway Foundation
PO Box 4561
Medford, OR 97501
(541) 774-6231

T. Klamath Falls & Klamath County, "Klamath County Bicycling Guide"
Klamath Co. Department of Public Works
305 Main Street
Klamath Falls, OR 97601
(541) 883-4696
Price: Free

U. Oregon State Parks
1115 Commercial St. NE
Salem, OR 97301
800-551-6949
OR state parks (http://www.prd.state.or.us/)

V. USDL Bureua of Land Management
    2890 Chad Drive, P.O. Box 10226
    Eugene, OR 97408-7336
    541-683-6600
    Bureua of Land Management (http://www.edo.or.blm.gov/)

W. Umpqua National Forest
    2020 Toketee Ranger Station Rd
    Idleyld Park, OR 97447
    541-498-2531
    USFS Diamond Lake (http//www.fs.fed.us/r6/umpqua/rec/hiking/trails/
    tr3_1460.html)

X. Oregon Department of Transportation
    123 NW Flanders
    Portland, OR 97209
    503-731-8200
    Oregon Department of Transportation (http//www.odot.state.or.us/)

Y. Eagle Crest Resort
    1522 Cline Falls Rd
    Redmond, OR 97756
    541-923-2453

Internet resources

- http://www.portlandparks.org/Trails/TrailLocations.htm (Portland's 40-Mile Loop)

- http://www.portlandparks.org/ (Portland Parks and Recreation - Portland, Oregon)

- http://www.trans.ci.portland.or.us/Traffic_Management/Bicycle_Program/ pdxorgs.html (Bicycle Resources, City of Portland, Bicycles)

- http://www.thprd.org/ (Tualatin Hills Park and Recreation District)

- http://www.oregonlive.com/outdoors/cycling/ (Oregon Live: Cycling)

- http://www.railstotrails.org/ (Rails-to-Trails)

- http://www.tripeast.com/greenbelts.htm (TRAFFIC is worsening by the day and leading up to an intractable situation)

- http://www.bikeplan.com/guidtrl.htm (Bike Plan Source AASHTO Guide Path Comments)

- http://wwwcf.fhwa.dot.gov/tea21/ (Transportation Equity Act for the 21st Century)

Colophon. This book was produced using the Linux operating system except for image scanning. The following list makes up the entire set of tools.

- Debian/GNU Linux (potato) *Debian Linux* (http://www.debian.org/) *Free Software Foundation* (http://www.gnu.org/)

- tntlite 6.4 mapping software (Microimages, Inc) *Microimages, Inc* (http://www.microimages.com/)

- US Census Tiger Maps *Mapping and Cartographic Resources* (http://tiger.census.gov/)

- DocBook 4.1 *DocBook* (http://www.docbook.org/) *DocBook* (http://www.oasis-open.org/docbook/) *Welcome to the DocBook Open Repository* (http://docbook.sourceforge.net/)

- DSSSL Stylesheets 1.73 *SourceForge: Project Info - DocBook Open Repository* (http://sourceforge.net/projects/docbook/)

- openjade-1.3-15mdk.src.rpm *OpenJade* (http://sourceforge.net/projects/openjade)

- \\LaTex, TeX (Web2C 7.3.1) *LaTeX Project Home page* (http://www.latex-project.org/)

- perl version 5.005, GNU Make, GNU Emacs 20.7.2 *Perl* (http://www.perl.org/)

Notes

1. http://www.odot.state.or.us/techserv/bikewalk/localmap.htm Local Area Maps

Appendix B. Distance Chart

Table B-1. Paths listed by distance in miles

Path	Dist	Path	Dist	Path	Dist	Path	Dist
81	37.0	57	16.1	13	16.0	12	14.4
1	13.6	50	11.4	60	8.9	41	8.9
49	8.8	31	8.3	62	7.6	45	7.4
76	6.9	3	6.0	59	6.0	65	5.6
37	5.5	51	5.4	7	5.4	40	5.3
17	5.0	69	5.0	56	5.0	63	4.7
27	4.3	44	4.3	14	4.2	48	4.1
58	4.0	38	3.9	26	3.9	28	3.9
16	3.8	42	3.6	61	3.5	43	3.4
66	3.3	46	3.2	36	3.2	67	3.0
21	3.0	24	2.7	19	2.6	18	2.6
39	2.6	55	2.6	82	2.6	73	2.5
20	2.4	2	2.2	77	2.0	64	1.9
32	1.9	6	1.8	4	1.8	22	1.8
54	1.7	79	1.6	52	1.6	75	1.6
29	1.5	34	1.5	33	1.5	78	1.5
80	1.4	25	1.4	53	1.3	30	1.3
70	1.3	5	1.2	72	1.2	23	1.2
15	1.2	10	1.2	11	1.2	8	1.1
35	1.1	71	1.0	47	1.0	9	1.0
74	1.0	68	1.0				